MY CHOICE TO CHOOSE

A Memoir

By
Christina S. Johnson

MY CHOICE TO CHOOSE

Printed in the United States of America

ISBN: 979-8-9909892-0-7 (Paperback)
ISBN: 979-8-218-41668-3 (Hardcover)
ISBN: 979-8-9909892-1-4 (eBook)

DEDICATION

"Friends are the family we choose."— *Edna Buchanan*[1]

Michelle "Chelle" Kennedy, my neighbor, best friend, and devoted sister, I dedicate my book to you.

We have laughed and enjoyed life from the sixth grade to the present day. You are the epitome of love, grace, and selflessness. I dedicate this book to you, for always being the person who has been the most consistent in my life. Forgive me for any time I have let you down or disappointed you. I pray that I have demonstrated love through my actions and loyalty.

You've had the same response every time I have called you in distress over the years. Whether it was me, my children, and/or grandchildren, you've always said, "I am on my way!" You have walked with me through this journey since the sixth grade. I know you have witnessed so many of the hardships that I speak of in this book. I know that there was nothing you could do as a child to protect me but thank you for being present for me then, as well as now.

Thank you for always having my back in great times and bad. I am grateful that you cared for me enough to love me through my bubble. Thank you for helping me to raise my children. Thank you for being their secret keeper when they couldn't share with me, just like you did with me! I appreciate you going to bat for them. We adore you. I don't know where I would be without your love, support, friendship, and sisterhood.

I love you with all of my heart and soul.

TABLE OF CONTENTS

INTRODUCTION

"A dream delayed is not a dream denied." Reverend R.L. White.[2]

Imagine deferring your dreams and then watching them dry up, fester, stink, and sag like the heavy load Langston Hughes described in his famous poem, "Harlem." I was birthed and raised under the discomfort and agitation of that load.

My mother conceived me when she was barely more than a child herself. I can't say she didn't want me outright; perhaps I'm unwilling to admit it. What I know for sure is that she put her dreams on the back burner to keep a roof over our heads and thrift clothes on my back.

The hardships in her early life shaped the woman that she would eventually become. She is a force — tough as nails and sometimes mean, but undeniably stunning. The woman is fine; I'm talking 5'9, slim-thick, with brown skin, full lips, and beautiful almond eyes. In her prime, she turned heads, naturally, men were drawn to her. I don't think she realized how good she looked; she was too bitter about how her life panned out to notice that she had it going on.

As a young girl, I felt the tension in the air, the silent whispers of disappointment, and the loud echoes of bad choices that lingered in every corner of our home. Even in my innocence, I knew that something wasn't right, children aren't oblivious to their caretakers' pain. I believed she loved me and mothered me to the best of her ability. Believing this was a conscious choice that I made a long time ago, and it freed me to relax my shoulders a little bit.

I am a firm believer that our origin story shapes us profoundly, which is why we're all intrigued by our ancestors. What they went through affects us today. We carry their joy and their pain in our DNA. The closer they are to you in your family tree, the more affected you are. Our grandparents and our great grandparents have plenty of influence on our lives, but our parents have even more. So, it should come as no surprise to you that the theme of deferred dreams has woven itself intricately into the fabric of my life.

I had dreams of creating a nuclear family, yet I too became a teenage single mother. After witnessing my mother endure years of abuse at the hands of my stepfather, I vowed never to follow her path, only to face similar hardships in my own relationships. Homelessness, health scares, and more adversity marked my path. But amid the struggle, I also had many dreams realized — like finding the sister I never had in my best friend and confidante Chelle, gaining global recognition from a reality TV stint, achieving success designing celebrity homes, and best of all, raising healthy beautiful children who have now given me the most amazing grandchildren.

My story is proof that dreams deferred are not dreams denied. It's ultimately our choice to choose. One of my deepest beliefs is that everything we experience is a choice, and for everything that we didn't choose to happen to us, we definitely chose our reaction to it. That reality can be incredibly empowering, but it can be frustrating too, especially if you don't like where you are in life. As long as you still have breath in your body, you can change circumstances.

I thank God for turning my life around, and I also thank God for giving me the courage to pinpoint the role that my poor choices played in all of my experiences. That was key. It's impossible to right your wrongs without taking accountability for the role that you played, even when it hurts, even when it isn't fair.

When people learn my story, their jaws drop. They can't figure out how I was able to go through all of that and still love as deeply as I do and smile as genuinely as I do. I didn't lose myself in grief. I used it to inch myself closer to the experiences that I wanted to have. Even when I didn't know what I wanted or how I wanted to feel, I knew what I didn't want to go through anymore. Sometimes that was enough.

I wrote this book to share some of the pivotal ups and downs in my journey in hopes that it will encourage others to start or continue their healing journey. We see people on television and assume that they have the Midas touch. We see people in our circles who are genuinely at peace, and it's easy to think that they have something that's out of our reach. My story challenges that notion — it's about reclaiming power and rewriting our narratives.

To understand the Christina Johnson that I am today, you must first understand my mother, Robbin Johnson. The first chapter of this book is written from her perspective. Her story is where mine begins — a journey of resilience, forgiveness, and the relentless pursuit of joy. Take a deep breath, let's go.

MY BEGINNING

MY MOM SPEAKS

They say life ain't fair, but that statement is truer for some than it is for others. I mean, I can't catch a break. Who wasn't having sex at sixteen? We all were. I wasn't like the rest of the girls I grew up with, though.

My biggest dreams weren't getting married and starting a family. One day, maybe, but I truly wanted to be a cosmetologist. I envisioned having my own salon and servicing everyone, from the plain Janes to the celebrities of the day. I imagined prancing around in the latest fashions, driving a luxury sedan, having a nicely decorated home, and living on the side of town with the best of everything. I was supposed to be the woman whom little girls looked up to — a role model they sought for advice, not a mother being asked for milk and everything else under the sun.

Yet, destiny skipped steps on my timeline and made me a teen mother. The song says, "First comes love, then marriage, *then the baby carriage." I missed out on the love and the wedding and went straight to the hollering, always-needing-something kid. Well, let me back up. He claimed to love me, said we were going to be together, and all of that jazz. I left home and my people eventually found out that I was pregnant. That was hard, but I didn't take it out on my child's father. I left him because I couldn't take his constant infidelity.*

I was a few weeks away from my due date when I stopped by his apartment and walked in on him and his family. That's right - him, another woman, and their son were together. She got up to leave as he told me we needed to talk. Denial wasn't part of my grieving process. There was nothing to deny. Anger, sadness, and a level of acceptance that I was forced to swallow were all I had. That, along with a child who hasn't learned yet that the world does not revolve around her, and a dream that I watched dry up like a raisin in the sun a little more every day. When I tell you life ain't fair, it's because it's not.

Love is what I'm supposed to provide the seed of the man who highjacked my life? What is love? From the time the doctors laid her across my chest, it's been a struggle to find those words.

Love hurts. It hurts! I don't know this amazing, unconditional love that people talk about. My dad abused my mother and mistreated me and my siblings, and she stayed. He shot through our house and two bullets hit my mom. She survived and she stayed. Was that love?

Did I mention that I felt responsible for the shooting? Yes, they were arguing because of me. Really, it was because my mom was protecting me, but in a child's mind, you automatically take responsibility for everything. Some years later, my mother was entertaining friends one minute, and the next, she was gone! She suffered a heart aneurysm, and I blamed my father for that for years. In a moment, my entire life changed.

To me, love is pain.

Most times, I love my child. In my own way, I do, but there are moments when I can't stand her. I can't help but resent her. I didn't get to graduate high school with my peers and couldn't follow my dreams. She is the beginning of the deterioration of what little hope I had left. This might sound terrible to you, but it's my reality and it's not for anyone to like or understand.

I'm used to being overlooked and misunderstood. It's like I don't even have an identity anymore. I desire to live a good life just like everyone else. I'm just a mother who's not supposed to have feelings. It would be nice if someone would ask me how I'm doing, ask me what I need, and tell me that I'm doing a good job with the hand that I was dealt. All I get is unsolicited advice and criticism.

Christina, named after my mom, was our family's first baby. I was the first sibling in the family to give birth, so everyone loved her. She was like the neighborhood's baby. "Don't hit that baby," they would say, with no consideration of the fact that she tore up my favorite poster.

"Don't ever put chemicals in her hair, she's got a good grade of hair. She's so pretty and has the cutest lil' fat legs!" It's like they don't even see me. Can't anyone see through my façade and into my pain? I wear a brave face. I pretend like I got it, but I'm screaming inside. All I wanted was to matter, to be loved and cared about. I'm just a child myself! Give me a break, I wanted to say. Then I got one. Or at least I thought I did.

I met another man who was successful in his own right and who accepted my daughter, although he referred to her as a bastard. I figured he'd help me raise her and give us the balance and stability we needed to get back on track. He even opened a bank account for her and started it out with twenty dollars.

Yes, he had a temper, but no man is perfect. Plus, I'm strong, and many would say fearless, too. "Do it!" I said, staring down the barrel of his rifle. "You can't kill me but once!" He didn't, and I didn't know whether to be relieved for another chance at life or disappointed at not being put out of my misery. By the grace of God, I eventually escaped with my life.

Life ain't fair and being a good person doesn't excuse you from being dealt a bad hand. I don't curse, drink, steal, or cheat on my husband. Do I get the adoration and respect that I want? No, but we both do our part. I gave my husband two sons, I cook Sunday dinner daily, I keep a clean well-decorated house, and I dress nice. We have a decent family, and, for that, I'm blessed. To be honest, my heart doesn't even have the capacity to be hurt again. That part of me is numb.

The only person I can trust is Jesus, the Author and Finisher of my faith! When I was at my lowest, He found me. I show my gratitude by attending church every Sunday, even putting my children in Sunday school. For once in my life, I finally feel safe. Within these four walls, everybody knows Sister Robbin is a good person. She cooks really well, makes the best cakes and pies, dresses nicely, helps everyone, and sings in the choir.

Outside of church, everyone is always asking me why I look so mean or why I never smile. What is there to smile about, if not for the goodness of the Lord that softens life's blows? It doesn't completely take the pain of my past away or my current pain, but I can repent and not feel guilty because I know God has my back. When I am given black eyes and called horrible names, God comforts me. I can go to church and feel better.

I do the best that I can. I wanted to keep up the image of a perfect life, but I had to sacrifice myself for it. I chose the facade of happiness instead of truly creating the life that I wanted. Yet I am still that little girl who doesn't know what it's like to be held, loved, and accepted. I just want to be seen and heard. I have a voice, and I have dreams.

As much as I would love to run and cry in my mother's arms like they do in the movies, I can't. She's gone. So, I am left to figure it out on my own.

I Chose Empathy

em·pa·thy

/'empəTHē/

noun

the ability to understand and share the feelings of another.

While traveling to Accra, Ghana, my friend Brely Evans and I were talking about my childhood, and she started crying. Even though I went through so many hardships, she was crying for my mom. She said, "I can't believe she treated you the way she did, but also imagine how she must feel after going through all the hardships that she went through."

The suffering and hardships I have gone through stemmed from self-worth issues which began from my childhood experiences. Part of the resolution of that trauma was attempting to channel my mother's perspective—or what I assume would've been her perspective—through writing in her persona. My mom was extremely strict when I was a child. When I was that young, it was hard for me to understand why my siblings and I could never do anything that our friends were doing. It was only later that I came to know how much my mom's trauma turned into bitterness, which was reflected in how she treated us.

I remember being in the kitchen and telling my mom "I love you" and she said, "What do you want? I know you must want something." I didn't want anything other than to let her know that I loved her, but because of the response, I silently cried in my room for what felt like hours.

Telling my mom's story from her perspective, and seeing everything being stripped away from her, made me realize that you can't give someone what you don't have yourself. If she didn't know how to love herself, then how could she love me properly?

Now, being a woman and experiencing my own traumas, and heartaches, I understand how much pain my mother must have suffered, not to mention how much our lives ended up with so many parallels. Having taken this walk in her shoes, I know she is not the villain of the story. I've learned to turn my pain into compassion for others who have suffered painful situations.

I have gratitude and compassion for my mom, dad, and stepdad. Had they not shown up in my life the way that they did, I wouldn't be who I am. I am so grateful that they were who they were to me because now I am who I am to my children, family, friends, and the world.

My compassion has given me the strength to forgive. I believe our lives are more blessed when we can learn to forgive and let go.

BLACK COFFEE,

NO SUGAR, NO CREAM

As kids, we would hang out at Eastland Mall, a popular shopping center in Charlotte. Long before Starbucks existed (in North Carolina, at least), there was a little coffee shop in the middle of the mall. Whenever I'd walk past that coffee shop, the smell would paralyze me with nostalgia and euphoria. I would just stand there for a few seconds, taking it all in. I didn't know why I loved that smell so much until years later when I overheard one of my mom's conversations. She was recounting her final moments of pregnancy up until my birth.

"I remember Grandma kept giving me coffee," she said. I froze. Was this why I loved the smell of coffee so much? More importantly, having not grown up with coffee being brewed in the house, yet still feeling nostalgic for its aroma, I must have been all-knowing when I was transitioning to earth. Although in my mother's womb, I was already conscious of what was going on around me. If that's the case, then surely I wasn't put on this earth without purpose. In my soul, I was convinced that I was brought here to do great things.

"To whom much is given, of him will much be required," says Luke 12:48 (RSV).[4] So extreme hardships were bound to happen. I believe that I was aware of that even as a fetus, and yet I was still excited to get here and get started with my mission. It was a choice we were all given, and I, like you, decided to take this journey and make it great.

To this day, coffee is one of my favorite smells, forever reminding me that I was sent to this Earth with a calling over my life. Therefore, my struggles are not in vain. We all have some degree of dysfunction in our lives, but when it hits you as a child, it can be particularly disturbing because that solid foundation isn't there. You have to build it as you go.

For my thirty-fifth birthday, my mom wrote me a letter. Sitting with friends and some family, I unfolded the paper and began reading. "Although you were not conceived in love..." Those words stopped me in my tracks. I'm assuming the letter had a beautiful ending, but I couldn't get past the opening line. My mind interpreted that I wasn't loved nor wanted, only tolerated. That stung, especially to have been told that on my birthday. I wanted to hear that she was proud of me, and maybe that was in the letter somewhere, but, again, I couldn't get past the first line. I still can't tell you what happened to that letter because I never saw it again.

I was told multiple times by my mom that she was a sixteen-year-old virgin when she had sex with my biological father and I was conceived. I was also told several times as a child that I was a mistake. An easier way to digest that statement is to say, "I wasn't planning." After their breakup, I was abandoned by my biological father. My mom said that he began to say I wasn't his child, and it was extremely painful to find out that my father didn't want to have anything to do with me.

Adults don't think about how comments that children overhear will affect them in the long run. Sometimes, the parents' emotions are just too great, and they think kids can't hear or can't comprehend what is going on. Now that I'm a parent, I can think of several times I have had arguments or conversations in front of my kids to which they shouldn't have been privy. We are supposed to be the strong ones, but in essence, some of us are emotionally immature and act like scared children ourselves.

Kids know so much more than we think they do. My father had a child with another young lady before I was born and my mom didn't know anything about it. So, she opted out of their relationship, and my dad opted out of my life. I can't imagine how my mom must have felt walking in on my dad with his other girlfriend and their son. This was more pain to add to her already painful story of watching her abusive father with her mother and then losing her mom at a young age.

My mom never really experienced affection and unconditional love, so how could she teach it to us? Hurt people ultimately hurt people, whether it's on purpose or not. Misery doesn't like to be alone and can cause severe bitterness.

I Chose Life

life

/līf/

noun

the condition that distinguishes animals and plants from inorganic matter, including the capacity for growth, reproduction, functional activity, and continual change preceding death.

One of the hardest but most liberating things I've ever done was accept that before my parents became my parents, they were people out here in the world trying to figure it out. They had struggles, hopes, and dreams. None of that stopped when I came along. They had to figure things out while also learning how to raise a child, all while carrying the emotional weight of a hurt child who had to grow up fast. My mother was seventeen when she had me. Of course, she didn't know what to do. But what if all of that was part of God's design for my life?

Before coming to this earthly realm, we made an agreement with our parents to come through them. Once we get to earth, conditioning automatically starts to happen. We're bombarded with everyone else's ideas of good and bad, love and hate, right and wrong. But what if our parents were supposed to show up in our lives exactly how they did? Could we have become exactly who we are now without these experiences?

I don't believe that God is a God of mistakes. He started with our births. My parents showed up in my life exactly the way we agreed that they would, and I became exactly who I am because of my experiences (the good and bad). We're here to grow our souls in specific ways.

Had we not gone through the experiences that we have, pieces of us would be missing. You are beautiful and uniquely made. If you're looking through someone else's lens, life experience, or snapshots on social media, you're building from a disadvantage. We all have work to do. Our duties are just different. Don't fret if you're not where you think you're supposed to be. You're on a journey to get closer to the new you, the healed you.

On your journey to healing, however, you can't skip accepting that your parents are part of who you are. As an adult, you get to choose your path, utilizing what part of your journey you want to keep or leave behind. What you were taught or conditioned to believe can be used in your own life, or you can leave it behind and create a new way of being. You can make your own rules to shape your tomorrow.

If you're ready to start the healing process, you must first accept that things happened just as they were supposed to. Blame doesn't change anything. Thank God for the ability to begin anew. If you choose to stay angry and resentful, that makes for a Bitter Betty! There is nothing less attractive than a person surviving in bitterness.

One thing for sure and two things for certain, you get to navigate where your life goes. You are an adult now, and even if you are led by a scared child who wants love, you get to choose your future. How will you navigate from this day forward? It is your choice to decide which direction you're going.

It's amazing how you can grow up and feel that you aren't being loved in your love language so you don't feel the love, but you yourself can be *full* of love and very nurturing to others (or not). We were beautifully and uniquely made by God to come to this earth for a greater purpose than some of us even know.

Your greatest teachers are some of the toughest individuals you have encountered in this lifetime. Find gratitude for your upbringing, no matter the circumstances, because you are who you are and have the potential to be greater because of the love or lack of love, affection, attention, or lack thereof. You were equipped with everything you needed entering this earthly experience, whether you believe it or not.

In order for you to manifest that gift, calling, and purpose, you must believe it, accept it, feel it, and open your heart and mind to it. Don't allow the pain from your past experiences to put you in a death grip you can't get out of. How do you do that? Heal. When? It's happening now.

Will you choose this day to start letting go of the past? You don't get a redo, nor can you change what is already done. The best thing to do is start accepting that those cards were not randomly dealt. That is the hand you chose. So, is it time to get down to the business of healing your past pain and trauma, or will you choose to stay stagnant and unforgiving, blaming others for your circumstances?

What the Devil Meant for Bad, God Meant for Good

One of the greatest gifts my mom gave me was introducing me to The Lord. She took us to church for every Sunday morning and Sunday night service, Wednesday night Bible study, Friday night prayer service, and Saturday choir rehearsal. We were also in Sunday school, in the choir, and on the usher board. I even remember washing feet!

Church is where I was born again at seven years old. While many adults say they were forced to get saved, that wasn't the case for me. I loved church, and I loved the feeling of peace and love vibrating throughout the building.

We're told from childhood to treat others how we want to be treated. So, we assume that we'll be treated well if we treat others well. We'll be loved according to how we love. That's not always the case. So, we're left with a choice: to choose bitterness and resentment or love.

Charlotte was a small town, so on our way to different places, we would occasionally ride past the tire and body shop that my biological father's family owned. I'd stare out the car window to get a glimpse of my dad. I would sometimes see his other children there with him working as well. Sometimes my mom would blow the horn, and I would wave as we passed by. Seeing my siblings out there working in the family business made me feel even more rejected and just not good enough. I'd wonder why I was never invited to join them. What was wrong with me?

When I was a little older, my mom would sometimes take me by his shop when I made good grades on my report card to show him. So, I would strive to always do really well in school, especially in my elementary school days, to prove that I was good enough to be accepted as his daughter, too. I anticipated those times to feel praised and accepted by him. He would hand me a few dollars and tell me how proud he was of me, and I liked the fact that he called me "Sweetheart."

I also anticipated the trips so I could look at him to see what facial features we had in common. I couldn't see the resemblance until I got older. I was told several times that he didn't claim me as his child, and I'd start to wonder if it was true because it just baffled me why a father would only be present for some of his children.

A few times, my dad's parents would have me over for a weekend. We would go to church on Sunday mornings and before the weekend was out, my dad would stop by and give me a few dollars then leave after about fifteen minutes. Afterwards, I'd return home to my family where dysfunction was the norm. Home sweet home.

The rejection was often two-fold. Every summer, we'd visit my stepdad's brother in Myrtle Beach. On this particular visit, my step-grandmother went with us. Once we arrived, we got out of the car, and she introduced my brothers to some family members as his children as I stood there, neglected, feeling like chopped liver.

I told my mom that my step-grandmother didn't introduce me. She said, "I don't know you either," laughed, and walked away. I could have melted. Although she was trying to make a joke, it hurt me so badly, as if I didn't feel worthless enough. I went to the bathroom and cried, wiped my face off, and got back in the game of life.

When children feel rejected by their parents, they end up with anxieties and insecurities that last for decades. Low self-esteem, self-doubt, and chronic depression are just a few examples of what you're left to battle. Some become aggressive, promiscuous, or people-pleasing. These effects don't end when you grow up and "know better." It follows you right into adulthood. Until you identify the problem and address it, it'll linger in the shadows of every relationship and opportunity you encounter.

Being rejected by your peers is hard enough. Rejection from your parents is almost unbearable. I experienced both. I would stand in the lunch line at school and watch the popular girls laugh and whisper about my clothes, shoes, and hair. I was called String Bean, Olive Oyl, Tweety Bird, and Big Lips.

I actually agreed with that last one about my lips. One of the ways I coped was by sucking my thumb. My thumbs would split and bleed from being in my mouth for so long. My mom would tell me that my lips were going to look like Donald Duck's if I continued, but that was a chance I was willing to take for that satisfaction. Plus, they were already big, so I thought, "How much worse could it get?" My mom tried the hot sauce, mustard, and hot pepper tricks to make me stop, but I prevailed.

In the third grade, I remember my mom would wrap my thumbs in *huge* balls of gauze. The kids tortured me with jokes. Eventually, I learned how to twist the gauze off before the bus got to school. I could then slip them back on before I got home. When my mom got hip to me removing the gauze, she started wrapping them thicker and tight as hell at the bottom of my thumbs so I couldn't take it off.

One day my teacher asked, in front of everyone, if I'd hurt my thumbs. "No, ma'am," I answered, "My mom makes me wear these because I suck my thumbs." I could hear the other kids giggling as I explained. She told me we had to remove it because there was no way I could write.

I also got picked on because I didn't wear the latest fashions. We shopped in thrift stores, flea markets, and attic sales by my mom's choice. She loved finding bargains, but her cheap finds were oftentimes my nightmare. While everyone else was wearing Jordache, Chic, Gloria Vanderbilt, Gasoline, Members Only, and Outback Red, I was wearing hand-me-downs that weren't any of those.

On top of that, my mom didn't style my hair in popular styles. Once, she pressed my hair perfectly and then curled it with the hot curlers you put on the stove. I was so excited. For once my hair would look like the other girls in school. Then she combed it all back and pushed it forward. I got called Diana Ross and the Supremes the whole day in school. I was so humiliated.

The ridicule and rejection only got worse. The day before I started sixth grade, my period came for the first time. My mom never explained what it was or how I should properly manage it. I looked and saw blood and thought I was dying. My mom handed me a sanitary napkin and told me, "Put this on, clean yourself, and change it when needed." I had no idea what was happening to me or how to manage it.

The next day, I could smell myself, and it was godawful! I went to the bathroom and cleaned myself with the hard, brown paper towels and hand soap. It hurt and it didn't help. Later that day, my teacher pulled the girls aside and explained what our monthly cycles were and how to have healthy hygiene during this time of the month. I knew the conversation was just for me. Humiliated doesn't even begin to describe how I felt, and I knew that I couldn't tell my mother because she'd find my fault in it.

If not for Michelle, that would've been a very lonely period of my life. I spotted her as soon as I walked into my sixth-grade classroom and was so relieved to see a familiar face. I didn't know her, but we recognized one another from the laundromat. We were inseparable from that day on.

My mom was too strict to let me visit Michelle's house, but eventually, she let Chelle, as I called her, spend the night at ours. Chelle had allergies and was asthmatic, so my mom would be sure to make things she could eat. I remember thinking she liked Chelle more than she liked me, but she was a great person—me, not so much—so I understood why.

Chelle also witnessed the dysfunction in our home, and it wasn't until my mom and stepdad had a bloody falling out that I was finally allowed to sleep over at her house. I was ecstatic. Chelle's mom, Mildred, let us laugh loud, be silly, listen to music, and have fun. Mildred worked in hotel banquets, so she taught us about etiquette and other things I wouldn't have otherwise known. They would even take me out of town with them. I felt seen and wanted when I was with Chelle and her mom. Needless to say, I was grateful for my new best friend.

Although Chelle knew the kind of hell that I was dealing with at home, she couldn't always be there with me. And she certainly couldn't protect me from it. For that, I needed someone bigger. I needed God. In his omnipresence, I never really felt alone. In his omnipotence, I knew that, with his hand over my life, everything would turn out okay. Plus, I was destined for greatness. I felt it at the core of my spirit. Merely knowing that you have a calling over your life lends you more resilience to survive the in-between time.

In my mind, college was the end of the rainbow. I'd graduate high school and then move away from all the constant reminders of how I was a mistake. I wanted to surround myself with people who appreciated and reciprocated the love that I showed them.

My parents may not have loved each other or the product of their union (me), but love has been one of the things I have always strived to give and receive in abundance. God gave me an overdose of love for people, even before I knew how to love and accept myself. The best daughter, sister, student, and friend, that's what I wanted to be. It fed my need to be loved, seen, heard, and accepted.

What I didn't know is that the need to be everyone's favorite was rooted in a void. My self-esteem was jacked up. I never thought I was pretty. As a matter of fact, I thought I was hideous. I walked with my head hung down, I never made eye contact, I thought my lips were bigger than my face, and I thought no boy would ever like me.

I didn't feel like I was good enough, so I needed everyone around me to prove me otherwise. This resulted in me becoming a people pleaser. It was hard to say no. I'd apologize for things that weren't even my fault and do whatever was necessary to avoid conflict. I prioritized pleasing other people so highly that I didn't realize I needed something in return from them. Any relationship that lacks reciprocity is bound to leave someone feeling used and abused, and yes, children as young as seven or eight can feel this way, too.

I felt like I had to perform in order to be accepted. I made myself into whomever they wanted or needed me to be. With God, though, I felt I could be myself. God didn't care how big my lips were, how I dressed, or what was going on in our house. That was the first time I felt "set free."

When I found God, or more accurately, when He found me, I realized I could mess up and He would forgive me. When things got crazy in my house, I would talk to Him. This may sound really strange, but I always felt like I was extra special to God. "Although God has no respecter of persons (Acts 10:34, KJV),[5] I felt that I had a one-on-one with Him like no one else. I believed that and felt it in my soul. Like we were really close before I came to this earth so I could feel His presence so strongly.

I always knew that I had a great purpose on this earth. I also knew if He could do something special for anyone else, He could also do it for me. I felt like we were close before I transitioned to Earth, and I could still feel it. He was my rock!

Religion played a huge part in our family life. We practically lived in church, which felt somewhat like a contradiction of our home life. Church was a break from the fear at home. Although my stepdad never attended with us, it was my mom's saving grace. It was her escape from the physical and verbal abuse she endured at home. She let out all of the week's hardships at the altar running, shouting, or speaking in tongues throughout devotional service, while I ushered and took candy money out of the offering plate. I might've been saved, but I was (and still am) a work in progress.

Sisters who went to the church convinced me to take a little off the top and no one would ever know. We'd go to the store after service and get snacks. They say the truth will set you free, so I'm coming clean.

Although I found my freedom in the Lord, I also found fear. I was told that if we listened to secular music, lied, stole, or used profanity, we would be damned to hell. It felt like everything fun was going to send me to the devil. I was so afraid to live for fear of dying and being tortured for eternity.

I was also told from a very young age that if I ever got pregnant, I would get put out. During that time, I didn't really even know how that could even happen. So much of the religion that I was born into was based on fear and not love. How does being afraid to live a great life bring you closer to wanting more of that religion? It doesn't. It makes you rebel.

I Chose God

God

/gäd/

noun

the creator and ruler of the universe and source of all moral authority; the supreme being.

Although I'm no longer religious, I still consider myself a believer. I believe that there is a power higher than myself who has been with me throughout this journey and with whom I still feel extremely close. How I connect with God is different today. I still attend church at times and pray daily, which is how I speak to God, whether it's to say thank you, ask a question, or just vent. I also practice meditation, which is how I have rewired my mind to release fears, live and think differently, and listen to what God has to say to me.

Even with this book, which has taken me much longer to finish than anticipated, I have been reminded that nothing is for nothing, and things happen as they're supposed to. There are no mistakes. Through the people around me, God told me what I should do. Through meditation, though, because confirmation doesn't equal courage or know-how, God showed me how.

It's so easy to get lost in the day-to-day routines that, unless something drastic and oftentimes life-threatening happens, we don't take that time to pause and check in. You never realize how busy your mind is until you try to quiet it.

Meditation allows for that time. Whether it's three minutes, ten minutes, thirty minutes, or however long, it's beneficial in so many ways. It's stress-relieving, but it's also a great way to recenter yourself. We are bombarded with headlines, opinions, requests, and responsibilities. It's easy to lose sight of God, our values, and ourselves. Just as fervently as I pray, I also dedicate time every morning to quiet my thoughts and hear what God has to say to me.

Affirmations and visualizations are also big for me. Do you know how many years I told myself that I was unattractive? That script has to be rewritten in my head and in my heart. My heart has been broken more times than I can count.

In order to continue believing in love, I have to be able to see it without seeing it. That's visualization. I just close my eyes and picture myself being adored, supported, and defended the same way I expect my children and grandchildren to be. Utilizing affirmations and visualizations is a reprogramming of the subconscious mind that has worked for many people from athletes to students to Fortune 500 CEOs to recovering addicts.

I've also done the fresh-pressed juice fast, the Master Cleanse for up to twenty days, and two forty-day, forty-night spiritual fasts where I don't eat. I only drink water. When I'm fasting, I can most clearly hear from the Most High. I know how I'm supposed to move, no matter how good or bad it feels. During these fasts, I've gained clarity about what is and isn't working in my life.

I've limited my use of social media when I am on a fast. I've dropped businesses and even friendships that had lasted many years. I've cut off all my hair, representing letting go of the anger, resentment, pain, and dead weight that had been holding me down. Instead of being covered in hair, I just wanted to be covered in love. These fasts feel like growth spurts for my soul.

Another way I experience God is through travel. The first time I was on a plane, I felt like I was in heaven. The clouds were beautiful, and the sky was so blue. Going to different places, eating different foods, and experiencing different cultures is a way of seeing everything that God has created. For example, being by the ocean is when I feel closest to the Most High.

I've opened myself up to all that the Creator is—not just what I've been taught in the confines of organized religion. You can still have a personal relationship with God and still have a spiritual community in the absence of religion. Do what works for you.

MY (UN)SAFE SPACE

My stepfather was born in the South but was raised in the North. He also experienced an extremely hard life growing up. He then joined the military and moved away from home. He eventually met my mother, and they married and had two sons. I quickly learned that two broken people in a union do not equal one whole.

Parenting was taught to me by watching my parents do it. It appeared extremely hard, routine, and unhappy. They pretended it was all good to family and the few friends they had, but they were more tolerant than affectionate with one another. Turbulent and combative better describe their marriage, with an emphasis on discipline in their parenting and a lot of church in the mix.

I recall arguments that resulted in black eyes. Whenever my mom could no longer take it, she would ask me to run across the street and call the police because we didn't have a phone at the time. Of course, my stepdad would tell me not to. I battled through the yo-yo of fear for my mom's life on one end and the fear of my stepdad getting angrier on the other.

Once, he put a cocked rifle to my mother's face and screamed that he was going to kill her. My brothers and I, afraid for our mother's life, begged for him not to shoot. My mom, however, kept asking him to do it.

I grew up afraid for so many reasons. Speaking freely about my feelings wasn't even a consideration. At minimum, they'd cut their eyes at me. On the other hand, there was always the chance that I'd be slapped in my mouth. Our beatings weren't always with switches on our behinds and legs. We had to hold our arms out and get thrashed on our hands and arms with my stepdad's leather belt. I dare you to pull your arm in which is a natural reaction. But that got you more licks. Then you were left with a swollen green-to-purple raised belt print that had surges of stings shooting through it for hours afterwards. There was always a storm cloud hovering over our home, but there was some sunshine, too.

Church wasn't the only thing that shaped me. I became a Brownie in the Girl Scouts and I loved it. I felt validated as a "good girl" because being a Scout was all about positivity. To this day, I remember the song, *"Make new friends, but keep the old; one is silver and the other's gold."* Hindsight being 20/20, I'm not sure after all the betrayal and loss I've suffered the Girl Scouts actually prepared me for real life.

I remember going to my guidance counselor once, in an attempt to talk to her about the turbulence that was going on in my house. I think I was just looking for a way to manage the fear and pain that I was feeling, especially not having my dad around. She pulled up a school picture of me and I was wearing my Brownie outfit. To this day, that is probably one of the nicest school pictures I've ever taken.

The counselor said, "Look at how nice your hair looks, and you're in the Girl Scouts. We have lots of girls that could never be in Girl Scouts. Look how nice and neat you look. You should be grateful for the parents that you have. You don't look like a kid who is going through anything." She wouldn't let me get a word in edgewise and sent me out of her office. I remember leaving her office puzzled.

It wasn't all bad. I longed for the rainy weekends when my mom would pop popcorn on top of the stove and we would watch *Hee-Haw* and *The Dukes of Hazzard*. Now, popcorn may not sound like a big deal to you, but when you live in a house that always kept a garden and didn't allow pork or processed sugar, you look forward to popcorn night.

I loved working in the garden as a kid, yet I didn't realize as a child how amazing it was that we grew our own food, caught our own fish, and ate so healthily. I know that foundation was set early and has always stayed with me and came back to me when I got off-track. These were moments when my family felt normal.

Holidays were a big deal. Christmas was one of the rare occasions to hear, "I love you!" I remember my mom and dad getting along so well. My stepdad would pull out his favorite Christmas album, *Bells Will Be Ringing*, and the sound of a record playing before the actual music starts is one of my favorite sounds in the whole world. He would play it while he prepared coon (yep, raccoon).

The first time he made it, I hesitated. "What is it?" I asked.

"Just taste it, girl!" he answered.

I loved it. We all did. So, coon became one of our Christmas traditions.

I feel like I became a well-rounded woman because of my stepdad. He taught me not to be afraid to get my hands dirty and how to fish. To this day, I can pick up worms and put them on the hook.

Employing his military training, he also taught me how to clean. He taught me how to properly wash a car and keep it spotless. He also taught me how to properly make a bed and how to wash dishes correctly.

To this day, I love cleaning. I only have a love-hate relationship with washing dishes because of the punishment we went through for washing them at the last minute before my mom got home from work.

He loved me, I'm sure, but he was fighting his demons, as we all have had to do. Some of them, though, we just can't shake.

The fear that was created in the household was so great that I was afraid to ask for simple things. Before I could finish one question, the answer was usually "No!" Always expecting the answer to be no makes you find ways to get what you want without having to ask, which means sneaking around.

I remember one of the first times that I was dishonest. The kids in my neighborhood were planning a party, and I was asked to bring popcorn and Kool-Aid. I was too afraid to ask my mom for it for fear that she would say no and I would get fussed at. So, I took it out of the house and gave it to my best friend LaKiesha. We ended up not being able to go to the party, so Keisha's grandmother told her to bring the stuff back to my house.

Talk about a nightmare. I got my butt torn up! I think that LaKiesha got in trouble behind it because she was mad at me and stopped talking to me for a while. That was one of the greatest lessons I'd learned about dishonesty.

Being sneaky felt like the only way to have a comparable life to my peers. So, when my mom would leave for work, I would turn on secular music because we weren't allowed to listen to anything but gospel. In the '80s, we listened to all types of artists: Eurythmics, David Bowie, Michael Jackson, and my all-time favorite artist Prince. There were so many movies and music that I didn't know because we weren't allowed to watch or listen.

Being afraid of your parents as a child is dangerous. Take what happened at Mrs. Walker's house, for instance. Mrs. Walker, a blind lady who lived across the street, was one of my mentors. She was where I could go to seek refuge. I would use her phone to call the police when the arguments got too bad at home.

Mrs. Walker was a retired schoolteacher who was blinded from complications of diabetes. She lost her husband from a heart attack, and her only son drowned. It impressed me how incredibly smart she was and how she was so self-sufficient although she couldn't see. She would listen to the soaps, read books using braille, listen to audiobooks, clean, cook, and bake. She spoke life into me and taught me so much.

Even though she was very independent, I was always there to help her out with whatever she needed. I truly believe this is why I have always desired to live a life of service. I always wanted to help people because I enjoyed helping Mrs. Walker so much.

Although her home was a safe space for me, it was also where I was first sexually violated. One of Mrs. Walker's family members told her he needed help moving something in her basement. She didn't think anything of it and sent me downstairs to help him.

He asked me to sit on the couch next to him and told me he did something with his girl cousins and that they told him to do the same thing to me. I had no idea what that could be. He pushed me back on the couch and took my pants down, then his. I was still very confused about what was happening and didn't know what to do. If I screamed, would he try to kill me? Or would he lie and blame me?

I told him he was hurting me, but he kept trying until he finally just stopped. I don't remember if Mrs. Walker called him or what. I only remember that I was shaken to my core. It always baffled me why his girl cousins would ask him to do that to me or why he would lie about them.

I Chose Silence

si·lence

/'sīləns/

noun

the avoidance of mentioning or discussing something.

I didn't think I could tell Mrs. Walker because it would break her heart, and I knew I couldn't tell my parents. I felt my mom would get angry and blame me. I also feared that my stepdad would kill the abuser, then blood would be on my hands. As a child, all of these things were going through my head. There are so many reasons that children choose silence when trauma happens to them. By no means am I an expert on this subject matter, but a few reasons include shame, blaming themselves, protection, and fear.

The violation in and of itself was already too much to bear, but the thought of having to repeat what happened—especially when I lived in a house where conversations about sex and private parts weren't happening at all—just felt impossible. I didn't even want to remember what happened, let alone bring it up again because I knew that wouldn't be the end of it. Inevitably, I would have to repeat the story (i.e., if I had told my parents, I likely would've had to then tell Mrs. Walker or maybe even the police). Shame is a heavy burden to carry.

It's amazing how the person who is being abused more than likely becomes a protector of their abuser. They don't want anyone to know what has happened to them and most times it's because they don't want anyone to look at the abuser differently. A lot of times when we accept abuse, it's because we feel that we need to be punished for something.

Think of that little girl who felt like something must be wrong with her because she wasn't invited to be with the other kids when they were at the shop helping Dad. She had no idea that grownups weren't perfect and that they had their own traumas that they were trying to live through. All she knew was that she looked odd (in her eyes), she was a mistake, she wasn't wanted, she couldn't do anything right, and she needed to be punished for it. Unfortunately, the punishment looked just like what her mom went through.

How could you be at fault when you are an innocent child? You have no reason to be ashamed. Even as we become grownups and make our mistakes, we have to understand that a lot of times it comes from the brokenness, the unstable foundation in which we were brought up. I'm not saying that makes it right, but we have our go-to escape patterns that temporarily numb the pain. We must realize what those are, forgive ourselves, and let go of any guilt we carry.

Children don't always have the knowledge or maturity to understand that they weren't in the wrong. In my young mind, however, I just knew I'd be badgered on why I even sat down with him in the first place. Why did I let him do that to me? When you're used to getting blamed and punished, you'll eventually begin to do it to yourself before your authority figures get a chance to. Had I actually said something, the situation could've very well gone in a completely different direction. But I didn't, so we'll never know.

In my case, I actually wanted to protect my perpetrator as a means of protecting myself. If my stepdad hurt him, I would've felt guilty. If my stepdad got in trouble for hurting him, I would've felt even worse. I also didn't want to hurt Mrs. Walker. She was like my guru. She had already suffered so much loss. I was actually at her house when her sister came to visit, had a heart attack in the living room, and passed away.

As a child, I was so confused about why life couldn't just be peaceful. So many things continuously happened around me. I didn't want any of that to happen. I'm not a fighter; I craved peace. Some children want to protect their caretakers' feelings. They don't want to hurt or burden their loved ones with what happened, so they choose silence instead.

All of this is rooted in fear. I was scared of having to rehash what happened, being blamed, and of blood being shed. There's also the fear for so many victims of whether or not they'll be believed, ridiculed, abandoned, or supported. There are so many reasons why people don't speak up about being violated. What's clear across the board, however, is that it shatters our innocent perceptions of the world. Life is another ballgame after that initial violation.

No one is perfect. I learned that very early on. No matter how old they were, people were hurting. As I looked around me, I was becoming more and more afraid. I was a child riddled with fear. Who could I trust?

Abusers Are Human, Too

I know because I was one.

They say the truth shall set you free. If that's true, then the freedom I've longed for my entire life is at hand. This book has been extremely painful to write and relive, especially my own mistakes.

When I was young, whatever came into my mind came out of my mouth, which was extremely reckless. When you behave this way, you often say things that truly hurt others.

I used to think that as long as I was telling you the truth, you shouldn't be upset. Why does the truth have to sting? It most definitely does not. You can definitely think about what you're about to say before it flies out of your mouth and how it will affect other people.

My mind goes back to an instance when someone made an insulting comment about my sister's appearance to me. I repeated the comment in jest. It wasn't funny at all. It was at the expense of the closest person in my life. The look on her face made me *never* want to do it again. Moving forward, I started to think before I opened my mouth and to season my words with sugar and not with salt. I was a hurt person who was hurting other people. I wanted company in my misery. It took me a long time to figure it out.

Not in a million years would I have believed that my bubble made me an abuser. What is "the bubble," you ask? It is my extremely comfortable housing that keeps me out of harm's way. I would imagine it to look like a clear pod that just follows me everywhere I go when I need protection. No matter how many darts are thrown at me, when I'm in the bubble, nothing can penetrate it. The bubble was also my life raft in my perceived sea of betrayal in which I was often covered. It was a home away from home that I built for myself at any sign of hurt, betrayals, whispers, funny attitudes, disappointments, and pain.

My discernment serves me right most of the time. I know when something isn't good for me, but sometimes the triggers would leave me thinking things that aren't true. If we are friends and I hear or see you whispering with another friend, I might think that you are whispering about me and then automatically shut down. I don't mean just shut down for a few minutes; I mean I completely go numb and my whole demeanor changes. I stop reacting, interacting, and speaking. I could easily go weeks without talking.

It was my defense mechanism as a child, growing up from the hurt and the pain that was going on in the house. I would be in my room silent, and no one even noticed. I would stop talking and feeling, completely disconnecting myself as if people were invisible to me. If I went into my bubble, no one else could get in.

I had no idea until years later that the bubble caused others to resent me and that it was a terrible personality trait. Yes, when I am happy, glowing, and enjoying life, I am the best person to be around. Once I stepped into that bubble, not even the closest people to me were allowed close to me, figuratively. I was there, but not there.

Once when I was in the bubble, an associate called me on the phone and said, "It's horrible when you stop speaking. It makes me feel like I did something wrong. You have a terrible personality." I was extremely offended because neither she nor I understood that I was trying to protect myself.

I started the bubble when I was little but never realized that the bubble could hurt anyone. I created it to protect me from the perceived pain that I felt others inflicted on me. Maybe I built the bubble after the molestation. I don't recollect the day it started.

My heart hurts right now just thinking about the pain and discomfort that I inflicted on others. I remember when my husband said, "I would rather you curse me out than to get quiet. It's painful."

I didn't realize until my business partner, and eventually, my therapist told me that it was a form of *abuse*. How could this be? I became the very thing that changed the course of my life, and maybe that's why I'm reflecting it.

It has been a daily battle to release that demon. To let go of what has felt safe for all these years. I think there's a difference between guarding and blocking. Think about a security guard standing at the door of an establishment. He's there to let people in and see people out. Now, imagine the door is locked and barricaded, and nothing can get in or go out. The Bible says to guard your heart, and I believe that is allowing goodness and beautiful things to enter. It also allows you to give love and wonderful energy out, but when forces come that aren't so favorable, you can keep them out.

A Question of Worth

A lot of times we block our hearts because we are afraid of being hurt or experiencing heartbreak again. Not only are you keeping love out, but you're keeping it away from yourself as well. We all need love and companionship, but sometimes it just feels better to stay safe. But are you really protecting yourself? Or are you hurting yourself by distancing yourself from being loved when you could be enjoying sharing a life with someone?

We attract what we need to help us grow. While you are regretting and feeling terrible about the things that have happened, they happened to you to draw you to your *greater self.* You are an amazing person because of the sum of all of your experiences, not just the good ones.

I think that people who allow others to abuse and use them feel that they need to or deserve to be punished for something. For example, I thought my father didn't want me around because there was something wrong with me. He punished me with his absence, so I felt as though I deserved to be punished by others as well.

My stepfather instilled in me that neither my mother nor my father cared anything about me because they didn't contribute to the bank account fund that he started. He sat me down more than once and showed me a Bank of America statement where he put in twenty dollars when I was a baby. He said, "I told your mother to take your father's child support and put it in that account and that when she has extra money, she should add it to the account as well." I saw that there was still only twenty dollars in the account. He then told me that neither one of them cared anything about me because nothing was put into the account for me.

For many years, I subconsciously didn't think I was worth more than twenty dollars. I never felt like I was enough or worthy of anyone to love me, to respect me, or to honor me in any way. Life sure does look different when you feel like you're not worthy.

When you see abuse growing up, you either become a victim, survivor, or perpetrator of abuse. I am definitely a survivor and a recovering perpetrator. I'm not sure if any form of abuse I've suffered from others was worse than the abuse I did to myself. My abuse took the form of constantly looking down on myself, talking down to myself, thinking the worst of myself, and betraying myself.

The way that you love in all of your relationships is the greatest lesson you can teach your children. Children don't always do what we say, but they do what we do. I was taught as a young person that love looked like abuse. That love looks like yelling, arguing, inconsiderate behavior, cheating, physical abuse, and pulling guns. I have understood for quite some time that we attract who and what we are and what we have or have not healed from, whether we like it or not. I've encountered not-so-good mirror images of myself, but also some beautiful reflections.

MY FIRST LOVE

His name was Eric, and he was 6'2 with a pecan brown complexion and hazel eyes. Eric played on the basketball team and was extremely good at it. I would watch him from a distance as long as I could until I had to tell myself, *"Face it, Christina. You have a crush on Eric, and he ain't going to want you! You're not half as pretty as these other girls crushing on him."*

Even my friend Julie liked him. We grew up in the same neighborhood, so it was a friendly competition that I thought I'd never win. Julie was so pretty and had the sweetest disposition. My self-esteem was nonexistent, and my broke-off-perm-turned-Jheri-curl wasn't winning any Best Hair prizes, either.

One of our friends told him that we both were crushing on him. Apparently, he saw something in me because he chose me. I couldn't believe it! I just never thought that I was an attractive girl. I remember him passing me in the hall giving me the eye, then finally coming up to me to say hi and let me know that he was interested in me as well. I thought to myself, *"This can only be one of two things: Either he wants to get in my pants, or he is playing a practical joke on me and everyone is in on it."*

My lips were twice the size of my face, and I was a total string bean, so I avoided eye contact—especially the beautiful eyes of the boy I liked. I mustered up all of the confidence I could to impress him. We started writing letters to each other every day and would walk each other to class after every period.

Every morning when I got to school, I would go to the gym to see him shooting basketball. As soon as he caught a glimpse of me, he would finish whatever play he was in the middle of and then leave the game to come talk to me.

Our first kiss was outside of the gym, and it was amazing. We spent every open second we could find with each other. Then the big question came. "Can I have your number?"

I explained that my mom was very strict and didn't allow me to talk with boys on the phone. I thought that we would break up because who wants a girlfriend that they can't talk to? I couldn't take the chance, so several nights I'd sneak on the phone to talk to him by having a friend call my house to ask for me. After my parent hung up, they'd call him on three-way then put the phone down so Eric and I could have our privacy.

My mom worked the third shift. After catching me on the phone when she wasn't working some nights, she started taking the phone to work with her. So, I'd get a friend to let me use one of their house phones. I would sometimes fall asleep before she would leave because she didn't have to be at work until almost midnight. I would hear the door close in my sleep, call him immediately, and we'd stay on the phone all night.

I was a virgin in the seventh grade and had no intention of having sex anytime soon, but I also never thought I'd have a boyfriend. Eventually, the subject of sex started coming up. Although Eric wasn't a virgin, he never pressured me. I started it. I had no relationship with my mom where she would tell me how to have healthy relationships with or without sex, and I assumed that sex was something that couples did. My classmates claimed to do it with their boyfriends all the time, so I figured if I wanted to keep Eric then I'd better do it, too. Our hormones were jumping like crazy every time we kissed, which was often.

It felt like someone actually loved me. Because we couldn't talk regularly on the phone, we missed each other a great deal. Eventually, we started skipping school to spend time together. We'd hang out on the city bus or go to Wendy's to share a Big Classic with our lunch money. Eric loved to talk and was very wise beyond his years. I hung on to his every word as if we were the only two people on earth at that moment. To this day, I call what we had the purest love in its truest form. I didn't want anything from him but the beauty and love he made me feel, and to reciprocate it.

Eric was my first love, first real kiss, first time skipping school, and first time feeling beautiful. Unfortunately, he wasn't my first sexual encounter. I was too ashamed to tell Eric that I was a virgin because I thought he would leave me, so I decided that I was going to have to have sex with someone else first to prepare myself for him. That's how you know young people aren't ready for sex, especially when they aren't educated about it. Had I known that guys love being your first, I wouldn't have *ever* given that privilege to anyone else but Eric. He had earned it by loving me so deeply and innocently.

On the day I lost my virginity, my mom's friend from work was throwing a birthday party for her daughter. That's the only reason I was allowed to go. I "slow dragged" (slow danced) for the first time at the party with a guy named Gary to Roger Troutman's song "Computer Love." Gary was kind of short with small, pointed ears and eyes that made him look like he was of Asian descent.

Gary had been around trying to talk to me, but I was with Eric and that was that. The night of the party, I thought maybe Gary could help me with my little problem. He asked to walk me home, and I said yes. I let him come into my room, then we lay on my little twin bed. I thought I would die, it hurt so bad.

The whole time he was doing this to me, I was picturing the face of every girl with whom I had gone to school who either had a baby or was known as a hoe, and I thought to myself, *"How do y'all do this all the time? This hurts!"* He wasn't gentle with me at all. It seemed that he was on a mission, so I let him finish.

A messy girl in the neighborhood who knew Eric and liked him told him what I'd done. Eric was crushed. He cried and told me he knew the whole time that I was a virgin, then I was crushed. Our love was so pure that we moved past that, but not before he was able to physically show me how disappointed he was with me for not allowing him to be my first.

After explaining how badly I hurt him, he said, "You gotta let me show you how it feels to be hurt." He said he was going to slap me. "I would never put my hands on a female, but you hurt me bad, Christina," he said. I braced myself, he did it, and it hurt. We cried together. I couldn't help but wonder if my stepdad fought with my mom because she constantly made foolish decisions with him. Did women deserve this? Eric forgave me, and we moved past it because we couldn't see our lives without each other in it.

The first time Eric and I made love, he took his time with me and explained everything. I cried before we started because I felt I had betrayed Eric's trust in me. He was so gentle and showed me what I was supposed to enjoy throughout the experience. He knew that my first experience taught me nothing and that this was truly my first time. Every experience with him was beautiful.

We decided to start chilling at my house when skipping school since my parents, who'd gotten back together, worked during the day. Along with my friend Audrey and her boyfriend Mike, we'd skip school quite frequently. Audrey had a baby at fourteen. In fact, she and her mother were pregnant at the same time. She took me to the free clinic for birth control so I wouldn't have the same fate. Her boyfriend Mike wasn't in school. He sold weed.

One day, Eric and I decided to smoke together. He talked me through the whole experience because he had smoked before. He was already a talker, but he turned into a true philosopher when he was high. We sang together, made love, talked, cooked food, and finally went to catch the bus to pretend I had been in school all day.

When I got home, my dad was beating my brother. My mom stood in my doorway with a look of curiosity on her face. I asked why Kumbi (my brother's birth name; he now goes by Kamarey) was getting a whipping, and she said because the house smelled like marijuana. I started peeling off my clothes, feeling hot and guilty because my brother was taking an ass-whooping that was supposed to be mine. I felt like crap, but while listening to that whooping, I couldn't muster the courage to tell them it was me who deserved the beating.

After that, everything started unfolding right before my eyes. My mom found my birth control hidden in my closet. I told her Audrey wanted to hide them at my house because she promised her parents that after she had her son, she wouldn't have sex again until she was married. Out of her own fear, I think my mom wanted to believe me, although in her heart she knew that was BS.

I also asked her if we could talk about sex. She said, "Okay." I sat on the end of the couch in our living room, and she sat across from me. My mother said, "The first time I slept with your dad, I had you. I've never liked sex, and the only reason I have it with your daddy is because I have to because we are married, but I don't like to." That was that. Unlike her, I enjoyed it, so I silently decided that I'd keep having sex. It had become my outlet because when I slept with Eric, I felt like time stopped. To me, it didn't feel like I was going down the wrong road. It actually felt freeing.

A few months after my in-home escapades with Eric, I remember sitting in church. A woman who rarely spoke in church but would sing this beautiful song called "In the Garden," stood up with tears in her eyes. She spoke in tongues, then in English as an interpreter for God. "My children, you have been doing things that are not of me. Stop now because these things will come to light and will be known. Do what is right and stop doing things that you know are not of me." That was the first time I saw that the Creator could speak through people to give you exactly what he wants you to know.

The following week, Eric and I had just finished having sex in my brother's room when we heard keys jiggle in the door. We panicked and started running around like chickens with their heads cut off. I heard my mom's voice say, "Who's in here? Who is that?" She was in the kitchen grabbing a butcher knife and was on the phone with the police.

Eric grabbed his clothes and darted past her butt-naked, and she chased him down the street. He later told me that while he was running through the park, he could see people laughing at him and hear the police riding past on the way to my house. That gave me some time to throw on some clothes and gain what little composure I could.

My mom came back into the house and put that same knife to my throat and told me she was going to kill me. With tears flowing down the side of my face, I knew I was about to die. I was more concerned about Eric's safety though. She calmed down enough to call my aunt, who was the one who kept our family together. She was like a grandmother to us since my biological grandmother died when my mom was young.

My mom told Aunt Ruth what happened, then told me she was taking me to Aunt Ruth's. I was so relieved. Before dropping me off, my mom asked if I was the one who had marijuana in the house. I told the truth. The guilt of my brother being falsely accused had been eating me alive. She also asked if the birth control was mine and I owned up to that, too.

My mom told me she was going to take the police to Eric's house. She said that he would be charged with statutory rape because he was seventeen and I was fourteen. I lied and told my mom that he was only sixteen years old because I didn't want to see him go to jail.

My aunt could talk for hours on end, and she did. I listened very carefully as she gave me a lesson to this day that I have passed down to my children. "Think for yourself." She said that she was going to take me to the hospital to see AIDS patients and teen mothers, but she decided not to.

After hours of talking, she asked me, "Well, did you like it?" While I was engulfed in hours of conversation with my auntie, my mom was at Eric's house telling his mom and sisters what happened. He had a very tight-knit family. She told them if she caught Eric near me again, she was going to kill him. When Eric got home that night, his mom told him what had happened and that he was to never see me again. We were forced to break up.

I cried myself to sleep that night and quite a few nights after realizing that the love of my life was gone. As the high school basketball star that he was, girls were all over him. He eventually moved on, and so did I, physically, but emotionally, I was crushed.

I Chose Affection

af·fec·tion

/əˈfekSH(ə)n/

noun

a gentle feeling of fondness or liking.

The affection I didn't get at home made me realize I wanted to do things differently with my own family. I didn't know that the heart could expand so big until I had grandkids. That is the biggest gift they gave me.

Having grandkids is no different from having a child yourself. It's almost like a surrogate. Some people are like "Oh, you didn't actually go through the process of giving birth" or "You just adopted this child. How could you love them so deeply?" To me, there's no difference. My daughters gave birth to these kids, but I love them as if I did. If they're hurt, I'm hurt. If they're sick, I'm scared. With my grandkids, it's a second chance for me to do things better than I did the first time because I'm wiser, and my heart is even bigger. It was big before, but it's bigger now.

Because I have so much affection for my grandkids, I let them get away with every damn thing. I'm still stern, but not the way I was with my own kids. I allow my grandkids to be themselves, but I get to guide them.

It's like a boat. You get to guide and steer it in whatever way it needs to go, but you don't stifle it. So, this is my second chance to get it right. It doesn't feel any different. It's just that you get to send them home. If I have to travel, I don't have to worry about finding a sitter. But everything else feels kind of the same. It's like my kids are grown, but they still need me. So, I still am there for them, sometimes to a fault, but I get to be an amazing mother to adults and an awesome grandma to these kids. I've got five now.

Being a grandmother is one of the greatest gifts because if there's something I didn't do in the beginning, I get to do it now.

I had an intuition that my oldest daughter was pregnant before she missed her period. She sat on my bed, and I could feel it. I sent everyone out of the room and asked her, "Si, are you pregnant?" She chuckled and said, "No, Mom, of course not." When you live in the house with women, somehow your menstrual cycles sync. I knew it wasn't time for her menses, but I know what my spirit said. She had told me when she was ready to have sex. I made her an appointment to get birth control, but the appointment was over a month away.

Roughly a month later, I remember Sierra's psychologist calling me, asking me to come to her office so that we could have a group session. I told her I wasn't going to drive all the way to her office so they could tell me Sierra was pregnant. I already knew.

As parents, we always have our hopes and dreams for our children and what direction we think they should go in. This is one of the lessons that taught me to relinquish control. Our little gifts from God come to us to live out their destiny, not ours. We try to control it and make it what we want it to be. I knew the two things that I wasn't going to do were ask her not to have her baby and repeat the cycle that had been started before my birth. I wasn't going to ask her to leave.

My first grandson, Tru Fighter, was born on March 6, 2009. He came out looking exactly like his paternal grandmother with huge dimples. I was excited for his arrival, and once he got here our lives got even better.

When my youngest daughter, Kalah, was nineteen, she fell in love with a young man and ran off and got married at the courthouse without our knowledge. I immediately went into "I" mode. All I could think about was that "I" missed the opportunity to see my daughter walk down the aisle, "I" didn't get to help her pick her dress, and "I" wasn't able to help her plan her wedding, and those things were stripped from "me."

I laugh as I am writing this. As parents, we sometimes feel like everything is a personal attack against us. As I've grown, I now understand that things happen just as they are supposed to. We all learn and grow from our experiences. I pray that one day I will still get the opportunity to do all those things with my babies.

One of Kalah's "best friends" was upset with her, so he called and told me she was married. I don't think he realized or cared how much it broke my heart to receive that news in that way. I think they were married one year and then she conceived a daughter. They decided to make her my namesake. That was such a huge honor, and I cried like a baby.

At that time, I was terribly sick again with another growth on my ovary. I postponed my surgery until after the birth because in the event something happened to me, I wanted to meet my second grandchild. Her name is Isabella Christina, and she has such a beautiful heart. A couple of years later they had an adorable son named Kató Wolf.

Today, I have five beautiful grandchildren. The youngest two gifts from God are Avery and Amaia. I love all of "The Littles" so much. I am so blessed to be healthy enough to run, jump, and play with them. It feels good to be loved by these young people and to be able to give them so much love and wisdom.

When Tru was younger, Sierra wanted him to call me 'Mom' like everyone else, but he ended up calling me 'Mawmaw.' That's what everyone calls me now, except Tru calls me 'mom,' and Amaia Madeline, whom I passionately call 'Maddi-Cakes,' calls me 'Mommy.'

I have grown so much in this lifetime. Being a mom has helped me grow. A lot of us think just because we are adults, we are always right. That is simply not true. I've learned so much from my children. I've become a better listener and problem solver and more compassionate because of their love and teachings. That is correct—I said *their* teachings. They have schooled me on many things.

My grandkids have taught me that I can't serve God and Fear at the same time. As a mom and grandmother, I worry about things that haven't happened. I pray and then worry, which is a huge contradiction. We hear all the time about how powerful the mind is. We create with every thought we think and the energy we put behind it. I have created "the worst-case scenario" syndrome as it pertains to the people I love and everyday situations.

For instance, if one of my kids hasn't picked up my call, I assume something is wrong. I think they are in danger or something horrible has happened, and I go off the deep end, making up stories in my head about things that haven't happened.

Learning to reprogram my brain, changing what I put in and on my body, and lowering my stress levels has helped me tremendously. Our minds have a way of making us sick. We have to get our minds and hearts in line because we have no control over the worst outcome. Even if the worst outcome is the loss of life, we don't have the power to change it. Is it not true that transitioning is a gift? When we understand that people are being set free and are blessed to no longer suffer, it helps us to grieve differently.

We can't deny the fact that it is extremely painful to not be able to see and be with them in the flesh. Worrying is such a time robber and joy thief. Imagining the worst-case scenario doesn't change or control anything.

Meditation has been a major tool in helping me to go beyond my years of conditioning. I am focused on knowing I'm worth more than twenty dollars. I am more than enough, and I am worthy of having it all. I am healthy and whole. I am not my past. It's happened, it's over, it's no longer my reality and I no longer associate myself with those old habits, situations, and beliefs.

Moving On

My moving on from Eric wasn't healthy. I started seeing a guy named Darryl, whom I would sneak into my room after my parents were asleep.

Sex was the closest to love for me. I craved the male energy so much, though I didn't realize it as a young lady. I wasn't sure why I wanted to engage with boys.

My sister-friend Chelle would come over to spend the night, and I would let her sleep in my bed. She was probably scared to death while Darryl and I would be messing around on the floor. There was something about having the presence of a young man holding me, or looking at me like they cared for me, that made me feel loved. That feeling was short-lived, but the hole in my soul that the absence of my father made was obviously what I was trying to fill.

At this point, I was fearless when it came to getting my love fix. After Eric and I broke up, I really just stopped caring about what my parents thought and what my grades and my future looked like. Sex felt like an addiction. I needed it to fill this void. I used to believe that had my father been in my life and shown up for me, this behavior would have never happened.

I picked Herm, who made me feel safe because everyone in school was afraid of him. I went for the underdogs because they were usually the guys who were funny and had game. A cute guy could always get the girls because they looked good, but a guy who may not have been the most attractive by the world's standards could win me over with his wit and ability to make me feel beautiful.

They would say the kindest things and be the most affectionate or the best listeners, and that's what I needed. I would feed off of their compliments like a mosquito on a human and would glow like a lightning bug at the chance to be held.

From one guy to another, I looked for that great-while-it-lasted satisfaction. Of course, self-esteem, self-worth, and self-love never occurred to me back then. I would continue this vicious cycle until I fell in love a second time.

Maybe it was a coincidence, but his name was Eric #2. At least that's what he called himself.

We were living with my Aunt Ruth at the time while my mom and stepdad were on another one of their outs. Michelle spent so much time at our house that she knew everything about my family and me. When my Uncle Tom would drink, he would take Chelle and me out for driving lessons. This particular day, Uncle Tom was bowling with his league and took me and Chelle. We were walking out of the bowling alley to sit in the car and two guys were walking in. He told me his name was Eric, but his friends and family called him Abe.

It had only been about a year since Eric and I were forced to break up, so the wounds weren't totally healed yet. Eric #2 was about 5'6 with pecan brown skin, light brown eyes and a small athletic build.

The four of us went across the street to the movies when the next thing I knew, his hand was fondling me. It felt so uncomfortable! Eric and I talked on the phone quite a few times, but one day I called, and he said that they had just gotten back from his dad's funeral and that he was eating with his family.

This was another relationship where I felt like I must save everyone in the world from pain. The young girl who was saved in the church, who wanted to live a life of service, was a people-pleasing, Ms. Fix-it from a youngin.

From the time I quit obsessively sucking my thumb, I picked up other habits: making money and evangelizing. I used my report card reward money to buy and sell candy (which, in retrospect, was the beginning of my entrepreneurial spirit). It was less about making money, though, and more about making my hungry friends happy. It was against the rules, but I couldn't deprive myself of the opportunity to be the one everyone sought out. I had what they needed. All the while, I'd tell those who would listen about Jesus.

I was like a counselor to my peers. I had an answer or prayer for everything. I even saved a little boy in the fifth grade. That's how serious I'd become about my relationship with God.

I've had a love for people since I was a girl. I never wanted anyone to feel the level of pain that I had felt in my young life.

A few weeks later, my mom informed us that she found a house, and it was right around the corner from Eric Number Two's house. Imagine both of our excitement to realize that we lived so close. It was about to be so on!

I transferred to West Mecklenburg High School and rode the bus with kids I had never seen in my life. When I got to school, I recognized one girl, Crystal, who attended another school I had been to. She showed me around while telling me how in love she was with a guy named Eric whose father was a preacher (just like my boyfriend's was), lived in Lakeview (just like my boyfriend did), and went to the same school but rarely came (just like, you guessed it, *my* boyfriend).

After I confronted him about it, he stumbled over his words, pretended that he didn't hear me, and then finally said he liked me more. I told him I knew her and that he had to make a choice, or I couldn't talk to him anymore. He was at my house less than an hour later. He chose me, and I fell so deeply in love with that boy, I couldn't see straight.

From fifteen to twenty-two years old, we were together off and on. Mostly on, but I would break up with him when I'd find out about the other chicks. I'd date other people until he got me back. He cheated on me the entire time we were together. He already had a child, and even his son's mother tortured me in school, telling me when they were together last or if another girl was over there while we were in school. He would always deny the allegations.

Although I was later given the nickname Shirley Holmes (derived from Sherlock Holmes), it wasn't my investigative nature that caught him. The women would usually find me and tell me of his sex-capades. This relationship caused me a lot of pain. I felt that I loved him too much. He never verbally or physically abused me, but his actions made me feel like I wasn't good enough.

I cried a lot over this one. I had never been alone without a boyfriend or lover since my first love, Eric Johnson. So, I continued sleeping with him while we were so-called broken up.

I kept a journal when I was growing up, which seemed like a pretty healthy hobby until I came home one day to all of my belongings packed in black garbage bags and the journals lying on the sofa. *Oh no, my momma read my journals!*

Although I was living in sin according to Christianity, I talked to God often. I'd ask him to please remove me from my house, however, I was totally unprepared when the opportunity presented itself.

I won't pretend that I was an angel. About a month before my mother read my journals and packed my bags, I had been babysitting a little girl from the church. I had friends over, and we were smoking weed, cursing, and hanging out. Young and stupid, I know, but I was a teenager in a lot of pain.

I stared at the two college-ruled papered, orange three-ring folders, knowing I was dead meat. The written words and memories flashed in my mind: my feelings, the way I felt about my parents, the sexual relationships I'd had...it was all in there. Then came the beating. I lay on the floor trying to block the hits from her pink flat shoe. I looked at the tiny nails on the sole of the shoe when it was coming down on me, feeling betrayed and even angry.

I was blinded by my own selfish need to be heard and understood, not realizing how hurt my mother was by these writings. I was going to live with my stepdad, my mom said. True to her word, she sent me there. I got settled in for one day, then she was back for another round.

My school had sent my report card in the mail, so my secret was out. I had been ditching school a lot. Along with the report card, she brought a tree branch and beat me 'til I was black, blue, and green. It was so bad that I called the police. They came and asked me if I wanted to press charges. It had to have been bad, because even my stepdad, whom I'd started calling my dad by this time, said, "If you do press charges, Christina, I will support you because she had no right to come over here and beat you like that."

I couldn't press charges against my mother. My heart wouldn't let me. The police called social services, who I thought would save me. By the time they showed up to investigate, I was back living with my mom. They took pictures and asked questions, but the scars were almost completely gone.

My mom walked out and said, "Take her on with you. Y'all can have her." It felt kind of like that summer we visited my stepdad's family and my mom joked that she didn't know me, either. This time was worse though. The social worker said,

"No ma'am, we don't do that. We're here to check on the child and report findings, but we try to keep the child in the home."

I'm dead when he leaves is all I could think. Needless to say, she didn't kill me. The verbal attacks were vicious though. Whoever said sticks and stones could break bones, but words will never hurt was a lie. Being called trifling and told that you'll never amount to anything felt emotionally comparable to being uppercut right in the belly. It hurt. Those verbal punches below the belt were one of many putdowns and letdowns in my childhood.

As a young girl, I thought if I could be the perfect Christian, my mom would finally really love me because she loved church so much. I strived to be flawless, but at one point I stopped caring to get my love fix. I have battled with trying not to crucify myself for being human, committing sins or mistakes of any kind. Again, it all boiled down to wanting to be *loved*.

I Chose Pain

pain

/pān/

noun

physical suffering or discomfort caused by illness or injury.

I was put down quite a bit as a youth and eventually put out of my home at sixteen because I was pregnant. Being a sexually active teen and then a teenage mother, I believe, was the result of my choices and my biological father's non-acceptance. I looked high and low for that male energy that I wasn't able to receive from my dad. As long as the resentment, bitterness, and anger were present in me, I was paralyzed. I was stuck in the same decision-making process of choosing relationships that would only hurt me but expecting a different outcome each time.

Resentment and bitterness are products of holding onto anger. While anger is a righteous emotion that serves a purpose in our lives, it can also be a distraction. When you're angry, you're refusing to accept something as it is. When you can't accept what is, you can't grow. You can't focus on yourself and where you went wrong. This applies whether you're a teenager or a full-grown adult. Underneath anger is pain and disappointment. I was dead wrong for skipping school, smoking weed, and lying to my parents, but, while on the floor getting beaten with that shoe, I was completely blind to my mother's pain. When I saw those black garbage bags packed or heard her tell that social worker to take me, I took it as another form of abandonment. She doesn't want me, I believed. I'm unlovable, I thought. When you're in pain, you can be blind to other people's pain.

That goes for my mother too. She lost her mother when she was young, became a mother after her first-time having sex, and was betrayed and abandoned by the man who fathered her child. Even considering her admission of not enjoying sex and feeling obligated to do it because she was married, my mother was in a lot of pain—pain that had turned into bitterness. Of course, she was blind to anyone else's suffering. She was hurting.

Hurt people also often choose pain. Just as my mother chose to marry a man who consistently harmed her physically, verbally, and emotionally, I followed in her footsteps, even as a teenager. Having dated Eric Johnson, I knew better. I knew what pure love felt like. It wasn't perfect, of course, but it was pure. It was real. From that, I chose someone who only considered my feelings enough to lie to me about his transgressions. He never tried to change his behavior though.

And, for years, I'd throw in the towel and then jump back in the ring to get it. I was addicted to the pain. It's as if I was on a mission to beat it. If I could make him love me and respect me, then it'd somehow prove my worth. In the meantime, the letdowns affirmed what I already believed about myself: I was worthless.

Between the name-calling from my parents and my own feelings about myself, those hurtful words were buried deep inside of me. This is another reason meditation and affirmations are so powerful. Meditation reveals the emotions that exist beneath the obvious ones. You might be angry, but what's under there? Sitting still for a moment might reveal that you're actually afraid or hurt. What are those emotions trying to tell you? And how are you trying to avoid this message through your self-sabotaging behavior? Who are you beyond the pain?

My Father Speaks

Before my transition, I turned my life around. I was clean, sober, saved, and teaching bible study.

Robbin would periodically sit in on my classes. We had our talks and I let her know how sorry I was that things turned out the way they did. I could only give her what I had been given.

I asked her about being able to start over. She said, Christina is grown now and that's impossible. I really just wanted to right what I felt was my wrong. I really would have loved to fix things, with all my children.

I explained to Robbin that my dad told me to keep lots of women, and I trusted his wisdom. I mean, my dad had quite a few outside children and my parents were always able to work things out no matter what. I'm not sure if they were happy but they had a way of coping with the circumstances.

He didn't tell me what to do after more than one of the

women got pregnant, though. Was I supposed to stop my life? I definitely don't believe he thought I was supposed to choose one. Maybe I should have hidden things better?

I wasn't ready to tell Robbin that I already had a son. That would've brought drama that I don't have time for. I care about both ladies very much. Don't get me wrong. They caught me red-handed. In my arrogance, I wanted to know which one of them wanted me. She decided it was over and we'd no longer be together. She didn't try to fight for me at all. With how quickly she dismissed it, she had to have another man in her life. She had to.

She moved on and eventually married. I did, too. I married my son's mother. Yes, I would come around when Christina was over at my parents' house or speak to her when her mom brought her by the tire shop. It's pretty awkward because I don't really know this little girl. I would give her a few dollars, ask her how she's doing in school, then leave. What else was I supposed to do?

Plus, there was no sense in keeping my life waiting. It was an uncomfortable situation to be in. I felt stuck between a rock and a hard place. Besides, she has a new father now, and he seems to be doing well for himself. It ain't like she's going without. She doesn't need me.

I was graced to have a conversation with my daughter Christina. She was able to tell me all of her feelings about me not being in her life. She even told me that she thought that her choices in men weren't the best because of my absence. I was her first male heartbreak and heartache. The love that she wanted so desperately from me, she never received.

I listened intently. I explained to Christina that I tried to come around, but her stepdad threatened that if I did, he would hurt me. I know she may have thought that was a cop out but imagine how hard it is for a man to possibly look weak in front of his daughter.

Not long after our conversation, I passed away.

I Chose Detachment

de·tach·ment

/dəˈtaCHmənt/

noun

the state of being objective or aloof.

Not long before my father died at forty-nine in 2002, we were able to have a phone conversation. After that conversation, I felt like it was my gift from God for him not being in my life through my childhood.

I had the opportunity to tell him how I felt about him being an absent father, and I told him that it had a lot to do with the choices I made because of my abandonment issues. His absence made me feel unworthy, and I told him that. I'd see my siblings working at the shop and being around him, whereas I wasn't allowed to.

He apologized to me, but I felt that he didn't really take ownership for not being present. He said that my stepfather threatened and told him that he couldn't come around or be in my life, so he stayed away. I never asked my stepdad to confirm whether or not that was true.

I remember my biological father coming to our home one day when it was my birthday. He pulled up in the car with his wife in the passenger seat and handed me a gift. I said thank you then he pulled out of the driveway and left. He didn't even get out to give me a hug or anything.

I decided that day that I was going to call my stepdad, "dad" for the very first time. That was the first sign of detachment from my father, even though we were never really attached to begin with. I decided to just be over it, which isn't the same thing as forgiveness. I didn't forgive him. I just mentally and emotionally moved on from him and stopped expecting anything from him. He would never be a father figure to me, and I figured it was in my best interest to have a shrugging attitude about him. I knew who he was, but I had a dad already. He could raise his children in peace. I had what I needed.

My detachment was a response to my biological father's detachment. He was totally emotionally unavailable. According to *Psych Central*, there are four scoring categories related to a parent's emotional availability: emotionally available, complicated, detached, and problematic/disturbed.[6]

Detached is described as the parent exhibiting "distant, cool, and mechanical behaviors, suggesting that they're avoiding emotional connection." Mechanical is exactly how I felt when he gave me a couple of dollars for making good grades, and it's precisely how it felt when he handed me my gift from his car window before pulling off. There was no love in that.

Detachment is a coping mechanism. It saves us from being disappointed over and over again. While it can be incredibly useful, if you aren't aware that you're doing it (or maybe even when you started doing it), you can carry it with you into future relationships. It can become a form of self-sabotage. You'll never have a healthy relationship if you keep yourself guarded and distanced. Every time you decide to love, whether it's a friend or a romantic partner, you risk being hurt, yes, but you also open yourself up to being liberated, expanding your capacity, and having someone who can genuinely say "I got you," and having their actions match their words. That makes the risk worth it all.

You Knocked Up?

Marc was my new guy. He drove a Ford Escort GT, which was pretty impressive at that time. He had no problem coming over to see me, and my mom eventually let him. I'd finally turned sixteen, my official dating age, but we never got to go anywhere. So, he'd just come by when she was there.

I loved the fact that Marc was so intelligent. That reminded me of my first love. Marc made the world sound amazing, even if he wasn't always telling the story in honesty.

When I decided that I wanted to commit to him, I told Eric there could be nothing else between the two of us. Marc and I built a strong relationship, but it was missing a very strong thing on my part: love. I loved him but not like I had loved the two Erics before him. When I truly fell in love, it shook me to my core. I became fearless, yet it would weaken my senses like kryptonite did Superman.

I didn't get weak in the knees when Marc kissed me. As a matter of fact, I felt his kisses were too wet. In his defense, I've never been a big kisser. One day, I was at work (I started working at the age of fifteen) and got sick. My stomach had been aching quite a bit. My mom took me to the doctor, and he gave me medication for nausea and vomiting. He said I had a stomach virus.

That virus lasted nine months. I still wonder why he didn't give me a pregnancy test. Nonetheless, I was pregnant, and my mom was the first to say it. I didn't even know until one Sunday after church when I woke from a nap and my tummy was sticking out. "You knocked up?" she asked.

A few weeks later, Marc came over to tell my parents. I was prepared to leave because my mom had prepared me for this day my whole life. She always said, "If you ever get pregnant, you are getting out of my house. I ain't takin' care of no babies. You gotta go!" So, when Marc told her I was pregnant, I told her I knew I had to leave.

To my surprise, she said, "You try to leave here, and I will body slam you in the front yard." She said, "Me and your dad are about to get back together," then she called my stepdad and told him to come over right now. He arrived in five minutes flat. Marc told him, too, because I couldn't speak.

More than my mom, I hated disappointing my stepdad. He really looked up to me and he would often tell me that. He told Marc, prior to the pregnancy, that I was his hero. I'm sure that he damn near cried when he left, but not before he said the words that most disappointed me. He said, "Well, you know what your mom always said." They told me they were about to get back together (for the five hundredth time).

"You know your life is over, right? All the dreams you had are gone. Ain't no man ever going to want a ready-made family," he said. As if that didn't cut deep enough, he added, "If you and yo mama can figure something out, that's between you and her, 'cause frankly, I don't want it in my house." All my mom had to say was, "You heard your daddy. You can go."

I felt officially homeless. I grabbed a few things, and we headed off to Marc's house to talk to his family. Even as I felt homeless, though, I felt *free!* My mom didn't stop me, and I personally took it that my prayers to God every night had been answered. He was finally rescuing me from that house.

I wasn't sure if teenage pregnancy was considered a rescue for anyone else, but for me it was. I felt that my baby had saved my life. I made a vow to myself that day that I would never choose a man over my children. Even if my children ever got pregnant as teenagers, I would never put them out. I started looking up teen pregnancy housing to find somewhere to live. No one had space for me at that moment.

My life is just beginning, I thought. I made a few vows to myself during that pregnancy. One, I set out to singlehandedly break the curse of teenage pregnancy on my family. I also vowed to do things differently than my parents had done. I'd keep what I felt worked for me. What I felt like was too far, like the beatings and name-calling, I wouldn't do when it came to raising my child.

Also, unlike other teen moms I had witnessed, I decided to raise my own child and not run the streets, leaving my responsibility to other people. I would start by giving my children something I never had: *self-esteem*. I also dreamed of one day helping teenage girls, especially pregnant teens with nowhere to go.

Staying at Marc's house wasn't comfortable at all. It wasn't like they were expecting to take in a pregnant girl anyway. His mom was cool. His oldest sister was also cool, but she eventually left and went to the Navy. They never kept food in the house, which was unhealthy and tortuous for a pregnant woman.

My worst memory was the day we went to Hardee's. I was so glad I was going to have food to eat. I got sick when we brought the food home, so I threw up and fell asleep. Marc put my food in the fridge, and I woke up starving. I went to the fridge to get my burger, and it was gone. I was distraught, extremely angry, and hungry as hell. One of his older brothers ate my burger and nonchalantly admitted it.

I called Michelle. Her mom, Mildred, let me catch a cab and come over to eat and wash clothes quite frequently. I spent so much time over there because they had food, and I loved being close to my sister-friend. Since I was banished from my house, I felt like Chelle was the only family I had left.

One day, I got into a fight with Marc because I wanted to spend the night with Chelle, but he wanted me to come back to his house. He kept grabbing my arm, so I told him very calmly, "Grab me one more time and we gonna fight." He tested me and I started tearing his head up. Mildred had to drag me into the house, clawing.

Mildred had been asking me to come stay with them, and I kept telling her no because I thought once she found out I was pregnant, she'd put me out like my mom did. Back in the day, if you got pregnant, parents didn't want you to be around their daughters (as if pregnancy was contagious). After this fight, Mildred asked me to stay again, and this time, I said yes. I figured if I could just stay there until I started really showing, I'd have enough time to find somewhere else to go.

All of the homes for teens like me had waiting lists, and I didn't know what to do. I applied for public housing, which was also wait-listed, and got on Medicaid and AFDC (welfare). I didn't listen to my mom and wait until marriage. Therefore,

I was making taxpayers pay for my decision to be a pregnant teen who would soon be labeled "mom."

I stayed sick in the mornings, so I would have to get up and fix myself a liver pudding (we called it livermush), egg and cheese sandwich (my all-time favorite at the time) to beat the morning nausea. I had been there maybe a month when I woke one morning to fix a sandwich before having to run to the bathroom. I turned on the tub faucet to drown out the sounds and threw up. I heard Mildred say, "Come here, Chelle." Chelle went in, and I heard the room door close.

I knew then that I would have to live on the street. Mildred asked Chelle if I was pregnant and Chelle said, "Yes, mama, but please don't fuss at her. She's been through a lot. Her mom put her out and she has nowhere to go."

I sat very still on the bathroom floor, scared to death about having to go beg my momma to let me come back home or, worse, sleep at bus stops. Finally, I got enough guts to come out of the bathroom and Mildred said, "Come here, Christina." I busted out crying and she said, "Come here, baby." She held me while I cried and cried.

"I don't see how a mother could let her child leave her home pregnant and alone. You gonna stay here with us, and we are going to take care of you and help you with this baby." I was so grateful for Mildred and still am, but I often cried myself to sleep because, as dysfunctional as my household felt, I missed my mama and my brothers.

When my mom finally did reach out, it was to ask if I stole her peach comforter. "Peach comforter?" I asked. "Yes, the one that was on your bed." I said, "I don't have a bed to put it on" and hung up. I cried so bad after that. My feelings were so hurt. I thought she was calling to check on me.

The next few months were filled with reading lots of books, buying a portable CD player and putting the earphones on my belly to play music for the baby, shopping for the baby, getting the apartment ready, and eating and drinking all that I could.

During the next phone call, I received from my mom, she told me that she was leaving my stepdad for good and asked me if the baby and I could come live with her. I took about ten seconds to think back on how my life had been up until that point. I said an emphatic no. I had so much happiness, peace, and freedom to be myself that I couldn't go back.

She ended up moving into the same apartments that I lived in with Michelle and Mildred. One parking lot down from us. There was one row of apartments between us. Unfortunately, in our family, we didn't have the hard conversations to try and fix things. We didn't seek therapy to work through our traumas. We just picked up and started moving on, while stuffing away and harboring resentments toward each other. Yet, despite everything, you knew in our own strange way, that we loved one another.

So, my mom started coming around more, hell, she lived damn near next door. Honestly, I wanted her presence. I missed my mother very much. My mom's beautiful smile is definitely a trait that I inherited from her.

When she smiles it makes my heart smile because it lights up the room. I'm not sure if she knows that because if she did, she would smile more often. I have always known how beautiful she was, I just wanted her to know. I knew that she was doing all she knew to do when she was hurt and angry, fight or flight. I would go down to her apartment to eat, and she would stop by and see us. She started to anxiously await the birth of her first grandbaby.

Chelle was with me every step of the way. She gave me a baby shower and was with me through Lamaze classes. Marc decided to go to the Army during the pregnancy, which was fine with me because he contributed nothing. He was in basic training during the birth, but he wrote me.

I'd started going to TAPS (Teenage Pregnancy School). I went into labor on a Monday but kept being sent home because

I wasn't dilated enough. My mother was with me the whole time in labor and throughout our last trip to the hospital. After the second or third trip to the hospital, she said "You are going to walk around this waiting room until you dilate enough for them to keep you." I walked and walked until I couldn't take it anymore.

They finally admitted me, and the labor process was underway. While in active labor, my mom was saying things like, "I know you wish you would have kept your legs closed now, huh?" The nurse said, "Ma'am this is not the time or place for that. If you continue, we are going to have to ask you to leave!"

My mom moved back, and Chelle was right there cheering me on. I was so relieved that the nurse addressed my mom because I would have been bringing a new life into the world with guilt. They moved me from the labor room to a birthing room and only one person could go in, so I took Michelle.

I gave birth to my beautiful baby girl, Sierra Symone, on Wednesday morning. I asked the nurses what day it was because I had no idea. They told me it was Wednesday, February 14. "You just had a Valentine's Day baby." *I just had a love baby!*

After having Sierra, I was able to get her into the nursery at TAPS so that she could go to school with me. This way, I could continue my education and make sure I had someone to care for her. I secured a job at Burger King that a friend of my mom's managed, and he would let me work until 2 to 2:30 am so that I could make enough money to take care of my child by myself.

Mildred and Michelle cared for Sierra while I worked nights. The only problem with that was Sierra had her days and nights mixed up and I would get off work exhausted, get home, and she would scream until the sun peeped through the blinds then she would fall fast asleep. Sometimes we'd cry together. Too often, I'd go days without sleep. When I did, I would have to sleep on the way to school.

Marc got out of the Army early and came home. He would stay at Chelle's, claiming it was to be close to Sierra, but he could never financially support her. I grew tired of the struggle back and forth with him to get his life together, so we went to the child support office to get everything on paper.

Marc was so busy lying about his non-existent work history, so I left him right at Michelle and Mildred's house because he wouldn't leave. I moved in with my aunt and cousins on the other side of town. One day, I didn't have money to buy milk, had spent every dime I had before payday, and my WIC had run out. A young drug dealer was over my cousins' and gave me money to buy my daughter a can of milk. From that day until now, I promised myself my children would never want for anything.

I was already a workaholic. I would work as late as I could then be so exhausted that I would fall asleep in my uniform on my aunt's couch, wake up, and do it all over again. Eric had been in and out of my life, so he was there for me while I was pregnant, and we got back together after Sierra was born.

He helped out with Sierra a lot. I took her over to his mom's house and his sister Taurus held her and said, "Look at that blue color around her eyes. Abe, this yo baby." If she has a B-positive blood type, she's yours. I froze! My blood type is O positive and Sierra's blood type is B+. He said, "No it ain't. She said that's this nigga named Marc's baby." She replied with a sarcastic "Mmhmm."

Meanwhile, I continued fighting with Marc day after day over his lack of support. Chelle and I walked to the store one day to get Sierra some milk. I was walking out of the store holding the baby when Marc jumped me as his brother sat in the car and watched. We had a fight over him not bringing her milk. I remember calling my mom.

My brother later told me that she said he should have jumped on me. I went to the police and took a warrant out on him because I almost dropped Sierra during the fight. After that night, I was finished with him, but the situation was just getting started.

I couldn't recall the last time I had slept with Abe. I thought it was right before I met Marc, but Sierra did hold a strong resemblance to Abe. There was no doubt about that. I started to doubt that Marc was her father at all. So, I took the immature teenage approach. Ain't nobody doing shit for her but me anyway, so what difference did it make? I'm her mama and her daddy.

Some childish ways were still in me, although I had to grow up pretty fast being a mom. In sixteen years, I never received a single child support check. He did buy her a rocking horse, a winter coat, and some clothes from a secondhand store once. I thought to myself, "At least he tried." Eighteen years later, when I got the summary of child support paid, it read zero.

Nine years after Sierra's birth, I married Lo. We sat down and talked about Sierra's paternity. Being my support system, he said, it really doesn't matter now because I am her father. He did step up and took care of the girls as if he was their birth father until the girls made a trip to North Carolina, and Marc asked to see Sierra to tell her he wasn't her father.

I believe her world crashed that day and there was nothing I could do to stop it. I apologized but I knew the damage was done, and it was my fault. Sierra being the oldest has always made herself feel responsible for everyone's stuff. She has carried so much. Her room was next to mine and Lo's, so I know she was exposed to a lot. She started communicating with Abe, but no paternity was yet established. Our immature decisions can be others' cross to bear as well.

I Chose Motherhood

When it comes to your children, you get to determine what type of mother you will be, even if the mother that you've seen hasn't been your idea of perfection. We have to understand that perfection does not exist. There is no rulebook on how to be a mom. But if you've seen a pattern go through your family multiple times, it's time for you to stand up and be the curse breaker that you were born to be.

I have a habit of shutting down when there's conflict. It's like I go inside a bubble and completely shut the world out. As a child, that was necessary. I was powerless, so that was my defense mechanism. When people raise their voices at me, I immediately shut down. A therapist brought that to my attention, connecting to an instance in my childhood when my mother literally slapped me deaf (temporarily).

She'd store some of her clothes and shoes in our closet because she didn't have enough space in hers. She had these royal blue satin pumps that she bedazzled with silver glitter to match an outfit she had, and I absolutely adored those heels. I went into the closet, put them on, and started walking around in them.

I know that some girls are fortunate to play dress up with their moms. In our home, that wasn't an option. She walked in and shouted, "What did I tell you about playing in my shoes? You don't put on my shoes. Take 'em off now!" Then she slapped me so hard on my right cheek that I lost my hearing for what felt like two minutes. All I heard was a high-pitched ringing in my right ear.

She snatched the shoes off my feet and put them back in the closet, and I never touched her things again. I also never gave anyone the opportunity to shout at me and get through to me.

Lo's former manager even pointed that out to him. He said, "When you start yelling and cussing at Chris, she can't hear you no more." Once I linked it back to that day my mother slapped me, it all made perfect sense to me. It also presented me with the opportunity to change my behavior or stick with it and just blame the person yelling for my shutting down.

While that might've been a saving grace for me as a child when explaining myself would've been viewed as talking back and being disrespectful, I'm no longer a child. I had to write a letter to my younger self to let her know we are okay now. I no longer needed her to show up with the bubble to protect me.

We can have difficult conversations and accept that it is absolutely fine to let some things and people go. You can't reach neutral ground when you shut the other person out. That's something that I had to, and still have to work on, at times.

There is something powerful about habits. Once you have conditioned your mind to do things a certain way, it is so hard to change. Learning that intentionally shutting down, not speaking, barely responding, and ignoring a person is abuse has changed me. I have literally taken time to rewire my brain through meditation in a way that I no longer look at things the same way.

Changing old conditioning takes a lot of time. The first thing you have to do is make the decision that you no longer want to do life like you used to. You have to make up your mind that you are going to change your old ways of being. Regimen and discipline are the most important tools that have helped me tremendously.

Now, let's start making new traditions.

My communication with my children was different. I was a disciplinarian during the early years of the girls' lives.

One day, I went to get my hair done and the women were arguing at the salon the whole time. I was there all day and they didn't finish my hair. They sent me home with half of my hair done and asked me to come back the following day so they could finish it.

I said in front of the girls that I was pissed off and they got excited. Although I used profanity since the sixth grade, they were like, *we have never heard you say that.* I realized at that moment, no more unrealistic facades. We are keeping it all the way real from here on out.

Vulnerabilities make others feel safe to share with you. From that day, our relationship grew. It was imperative that they had the freedom to share things with me. I would never want them to be violated and not be able to tell me. I also learned early on to put them in therapy because if they couldn't tell me something, I would want them to be able to communicate it to someone who could be trusted.

As mothers, we want to give our all to our kids. We have to remember that we can't pour from an empty cup. Make sure you're taking care of yourself too.

If there were things I did incorrectly with my kids, I had a second chance to get it right with my grandkids.

I'M (NOT) GETTING MARRIED!

At eighteen, I was working at a men's shoe store called 'Men's Name Brand Shoes.' I loved working with people. Even in the fast-food industry, I thrived. One day this guy named Stan, who was a friend of Chelle's cousin's husband, Carl, came by my job to pick up something for Carl.

The next thing I know, I was getting a call from Carl saying that Stan said he was speechless when he saw me. He didn't say much, but I didn't think anything of it. Carl said, "Stan don't get quiet over women." His brother Michael was shocked to hear that and said, "I have to meet this woman." Carl asked me if he could give my number to Michael, who lived in Atlanta. I said yes.

Initially, I don't remember asking Carl, or Mike, for that matter, his age. We talked on the phone about our lives, past and present. Mine was a little shorter than his because I was eighteen. I eventually found out he was ten years older. After talking on the phone about books, philosophy, and his love for art and wine, he asked me what I did and what my plans were.

He really wanted to meet the woman who shut his brother

down because that had never happened. Finally, he asked me out on a date. I said yes because he intrigued me. He made me feel mature, like a woman, through conversation alone. Nothing intimate, just great conversation.

He picked me up for dinner in a suit and took me to a beautiful restaurant overlooking the lake. I felt so special, so beautiful, and so honored to be there with him. Michael asked for a chardonnay off of the wine list and explained to me which wines complemented which foods.

The waiter brought him a taste of the wine he requested. He did a spin of the wine around his glass and had a whole conversation about the wine with the waiter. I was so impressed. I remember having chicken that he paired with the wine while Michael explained his interpretation of the art hanging in the restaurant. He described the color and its meaning, the signature of the artist, and the number under the artist's name, 1/50. There were 50 copies of the art and that was the first. I was very attentive.

I don't know why, but he thought that I was bored and having an awful time, but I was feeling quite awkward thinking, *"I could get used to this, but do I fit into this lifestyle?"* Then I remembered that I have never fit in, and I started to feel even more weird.

After dinner, we walked around the lake and talked for a while. It was the absolute best date I had ever been on. In hindsight, it was only the second real date I had been on. Sex doesn't equate to a date. Neither does Waffle House. For me, being so young and uneducated in this area, sex equaled love.

Once he dropped me off back at my place, I invited him in for a while. We sat on the couch and talked for a little bit. When he got ready to go back to his hotel room, he took his herringbone necklace off and put it around my neck. I was shocked and confused. He said, "If we never get the opportunity to go out on another date, I would like you to have this to remember me by." I had already decided that we would go out again when he showed up on time in a suit.

From there, we started dating exclusively. Valentine's Day was coming up, and Michael challenged me to a friendly competition. We had to come up with the most creative gifts for each other. Then he would come get me and we would exchange gifts in Atlanta. I was like, *"This will be easy! I will blow his mind with this one."*

Looking back, my creative skills were nowhere near what they ultimately would become. I decided I would get an oil painting done of myself. Now that I think about it, that may have seemed vain. I just thought he loved me, so of course he wanted to look at me daily. Well, he pretended to love it even if he didn't.

Now his gift to me was amazing. He gave me a plant that represented the love and growth in our relationship. He told me we would nurture, love it, and keep it alive. He told me to dig my hands in the soil, and there I found an American Express gold card. My heart leaped for all of this because it was so thoughtful. I had never been loved and respected on this level. Keep in mind I was nineteen years old.

He made me a beautiful dinner, a whole Maine lobster and gave me a lesson on how to eat it. I was impressed until I started tugging at this plastic bag. I was mortified. What is coming out of this lobster? He seemed just as confused as I was. We pulled it out, opened it, and he was down on one knee. I was shocked. *Yes! I'm getting married!*

Not long after Mike proposed, I was back in Charlotte working at Men's Name Brand Shoes, when two men wearing masks ran into the store with guns and asked the manager to open the register. They proceeded to ask me and the manager who was a short and tiny Caucasian woman to get on the floor and keep our heads down.

They cleaned out the register and started emptying our purses. As they are going through my purse. I am watching them, and I hear one of them say, "Put your head down baby." At that moment, I knew they weren't going to kill me. I was shaken! My hands always used to shake from me being fearful as a child. This was a new level of fear. Needless to say, I quit that job because my nerves were too bad to go back.

Michael asked me to come to Atlanta to visit. I went there for a weekend and loved it. Not long after, against my family's wishes, I went ahead and moved to Atlanta. My one-year-old daughter, Sierra, and I moved into Mike's one-bedroom apartment right by Six Flags.

It was contemporarily decorated with minimalist taste. There was a sunroom that housed the glass dining room table and live plants and a small kitchen with a bar that overlooked the living room with no furniture but a fireplace. We slept by that fireplace often after my daughter was put to bed for the night.

He had a huge waterbed, but that was for sleeping, not making love. Michael had been celibate for two years prior to our meeting, so sex wasn't his drive. He wanted to dedicate himself to someone, and that someone was me.

Being nineteen, I wasn't quite ready to be a wife just yet. I wasn't sure that Mike was who I was supposed to marry because I was so young, still learning my way and finding out who I was. Having a child young doesn't mean that you know all there is to know about life. As a matter of fact, it can slow down the process of you getting to know yourself because that child becomes your priority.

Living with Mike was a confusing time for me because I cared for him deeply, but I was incredibly homesick and lonely. He worked full-time and worked out a lot. We did spend time together when he got home from the gym in the evenings and on the weekends, but I didn't know anyone else outside of a few people Mike introduced me to.

One day, his brother came by, but I didn't feel comfortable letting him in because he was a man and Mike wasn't home. I addressed him at the door and told him what time Mike was getting off and told him he could come back then. I thought it was odd since Mike's schedule didn't change.

Not long after that, I told Mike that I wanted to go home because I was homesick. He took it very hard. My heart was heavy for hurting him, but I also felt so crappy being unhappy in a state without my sister, especially. What made it even harder was that I was pregnant by him with my second child. Michael never abandoned me, though.

Mike took Sierra and me home. Not long after that, my Mildred, Carl, his wife, and Mike's brother got together in Atlanta and tore me a new one verbally. They told him I was with my ex-boyfriend when I got back to Charlotte. They all said that I was using him, that I was cheating on him, and that the baby wasn't his.

His brother went on to say that he thought I was having an affair because he came over one day and I wouldn't let him in. I would never have another man in my man's house. Plus, I was totally satisfied with Mike. I didn't know a soul in Atlanta. So, of course, my child wasn't claimed by his side of the family.

I think his mom saw her a few times when Mike took her over, but they never called or contacted us to be a part of her life. It hurt me so badly, not because of his family, but because of mine. Mildred was my family. She rescued me when I was pregnant with Sierra. I have always suffered from the root of betrayal, so this didn't help me in my healing process at all. I was reminded once again that it was all for one and one for all; me and my children are all I have. *"No one really loves me,"* I told myself. *"They are just in your life for whatever reason they choose to be, even if it's to keep you down and talk about you."*

In true "brush things under the rug fashion," we all moved on and now it was time for the arrival of Kalah Shanielle. Kalah was so excited to get here that my labor started, and I called my mom to take me to the hospital. It may have been a total of four hours. My mom answered and said, "Are you sure you ready remem..." I interrupted, *"Mom,* I am ready."

We got to the hospital with enough time to get admitted and prepped. On the first push, her head came out, and by the second push, she was fully out. Kalah actually had to stay in the hospital because she had a rapid heartbeat. It was one of the longest weeks of my life. After going home, I started to feel not so much like myself. It was my first experience with post-partum depression. I wouldn't have made it if it were not for Mildred and Chelle.

They ended up keeping Kalah for a while so I could get myself together. Postpartum is extremely difficult to manage. I couldn't imagine having gone through that without a support system. My mom would get the girls a lot. Eventually, my mom asked me for custody of my girls. I said an emphatic no. I know that my mom's intentions were good and I love my mom, but I couldn't imagine the girls being raised like me. I may not have been raising them to her standards, but these were my gifts from God and I wanted to raise them my way, imperfections, and all.

Mike and I had a good co-parenting relationship and continued to see each other off and on until I finally let go and told him that we weren't going to be together. He deserved to be with someone who was in love with him.

He ended up meeting a woman, whom my sister didn't care for, but I got along great with her over the phone. Things changed when I met her in person, though. I took the girls to their apartment to drop them off and I remember her opening the door obviously not expecting what she saw. I felt things between us change at that moment. I used their bathroom and left with my friends, who were waiting in the car with my sister.

Mike seemed to be happy, so I was happy for him. Mike would stay away for long periods of time, and I was getting frustrated with the type of father I felt he was becoming. You can start a new relationship, but don't leave your children out. The kids started complaining about his new love being mean to them.

I talked to Mike about it. I told him that her heart wasn't right and that she wasn't a nice person. He said no one in his family liked her either, but she was raised in a private school, so she didn't know how to get along with people. He constantly made excuses for her behavior.

The last time my children came home and told me she was mean to them, I told him, "I don't know what she was saying to my children, but you better talk to her or I'm coming over there to blow that house up." He said, "Okay, I know, I know." And that was the last time we talked until over ten years later.

I tried calling him, and his number was disconnected. I went to his job, but he was no longer employed there. I was so blown away. The one man whom I finally convinced myself was a good man and who had integrity in my mind was now gone.

I Chose Retraction

re·trac·tion

/rə'trakSH(ə)n/

noun

a withdrawal of a statement, accusation, or undertaking.

Yes, I changed my mind about getting married to Mike. I had so much growing and learning to do and although I knew that he was in love with me, I didn't feel that I was ready. I was still a teenager when we met and he was 10 years older.

As much as I would have wanted to be the perfect wife for him, I still had so much trauma that I needed to heal from. He was so mature emotionally and I just wasn't there yet. I know that I broke his heart.

We all have the right to change our minds. I knew that it was the best choice for us both. He ended up marrying and having two beautiful children. Although everyone may have an opinion about your journey, it is yours and you have the right to choose what is best for you. It ultimately ends up a blessing to everyone involved when your intentions are clearly good. I was in no way the perfect girlfriend. I knew I wasn't ready and

I didn't want to ruin his life. I knew that he deserved to be loved correctly, and my void would give him that opportunity.

We can make a decision and then the circumstances that we agreed to can change and it changes everything. Changing your mind takes courage because it requires you to be true to yourself about what is best for you. You shouldn't betray yourself no matter what. You must love yourself enough to make choices that are best for you and your life. Always be honest with yourself about what you really want the outcome of this particular part of your life to be.

It is okay to have to do things differently. Change can be good and can grow you because you are now taking accountability and responsibility for your journey. You deserve The Most High's absolute best for you. Stop settling for less than you deserve. Why can't it happen for you? It most definitely can.

Mike was the fairytale that I had waited for, but I wasn't equipped with what I needed to maintain that relationship. I was young, broken, and lost. Mike was an awesome man, an artist, a seer, and very intelligent. I saw all of that in him immediately. I was angry with him when he disappeared.

Kalah was crazy about her dad, and she was confused about why he disappeared. All I could think about was the rejection that I suffered not having my dad. I was crushed for her. We all have our life challenges and circumstances that we have to grow through. As I got older, I stopped accepting cliches as facts. I could only experience people and draw my own conclusions from there.

I had met some really nice men who weren't out to get you, who really did love and respect their family. Every person walking this earth isn't the same. I don't care if they are the same race or creed or came out of the same womb. "All men are dogs," didn't fly with me anymore. I learned to give grace.

I had pretty much been betrayed by every man in my life, but I never wanted to emasculate them or make them feel less than. I really just desired for someone to show me that all the examples I had seen growing up were not the status quo. Mike did that, but after his disappearance, I had to keep looking.

You Think You Cute

At 21, I started my journey of healing myself. I realized that I was hurt on a level that I couldn't reach on my own. I needed God, and I needed him in a way that I hadn't yet experienced in the church or growing up with my parents.

As they say, when the student is ready, the teacher appears. One of my biological father's brothers owned a herbal store in Charlotte that sold incense and various herbs for natural healing. We'd talk, and I remember him being so proud and excited that I got it.

We discussed the fact that we can heal ourselves, that God lives in us, that Black people are the original people, that we are in a constant state of manifesting whether we're conscious of it or not, that we are as connected to the trees as we are the ocean, and the person walking by us in the airport.

We're all connected. That resonated very deeply in me and clicked almost immediately because I innately knew and felt this already. Mike, my youngest daughter Kalah's father, had already introduced me to so much of it, but, even then, it wasn't hard to believe it. It was already in me.

I remember Mike and I reading *How to Eat to Live* by Elijah Muhammad. It listed all the foods that we should and shouldn't eat, how our foods affect our minds and bodies, and even how often we should eat. We started researching herbs and using healing herbs to heal our bodies. Our prevalent options seemed to be everything that wasn't good for us.

The words stuck with you long after you closed the book and made you take a closer look at the world around you (e.g., the types of restaurants and food options that were available in most Black neighborhoods and how commercials around fast food, candy, and soda targeted the most vulnerable population—our children).

Most of this information is common sense today, but this book was written in the 1960s, and I was learning about this information in the late '80s and early '90s, when most Black people were not having these conversations. I didn't do a 180 with my diet, but I definitely started noticing and caring more about what I fed my mind and my body.

My uncle Buddy also introduced me to meditating. I'd sit in a chair or sit down comfortably cross-legged, close my eyes, and do my best to quiet my mind. This practice taught me how busy my mind was.

I read somewhere once that we have about six to seven thoughts per minute. Some of us have even more than that. While it seems natural, it's not. We've been conditioned to constantly be on the go, constantly thinking of what happened, what we would've or should've done differently, what's about to happen, what's next, how are we being perceived, what's for dinner, how can we make more money, etc. Our thoughts are overridden with anxiety and want.

Meditation doesn't completely stop you from doing that, but it makes you aware of it. That awareness is key to learning how to let go, how to surrender, and how to find more peace in your everyday moments despite what's going on around you.

Meditation also gives you the heightened ability to put yourself in other people's shoes and realize that their actions really have nothing to do with you.

I started rationalizing my feelings towards my parents. I felt so deprived, and it had nothing to do with not wearing name brands. We were clothed, fed, and sheltered, but we didn't feel a whole lot of love. With the two of them constantly fighting like cats and dogs, we didn't even get to witness it.

Hugs, kisses, just asking how our day went without checking for trouble, and being told we were loved or appreciated or that they were proud of us didn't happen. Sometimes it seemed we were only acknowledged when we had done something wrong.

It wasn't all bad, don't get me wrong. But a lot of it was hurtful, including being put out after learning that I was pregnant. That was never addressed again, never apologized for, nothing. None of it was.

A lot of decisions that I made in my teenage and early adult life were centered on that hurt, that void. The fact of the matter was that I couldn't change it. It was the past. I couldn't change my parents and make them apologize or start loving me the way I wanted to be loved. That wasn't reality.

Through meditation, I started rationalizing. Think of it this way: if I don't know how to change a tire and my son asks me to show him how, I wouldn't be able to because I don't know how. It's not that I don't want to. I just can't. I don't have the literal or figurative tools to do so. You can't teach people something you don't have wisdom for.

I started looking at my upbringing like that. My mom, my stepdad, and even my biological dad did their best with the tools they had. They couldn't teach me how to love in a way that was patient, kind, forgiving, and holistically present if they were never taught. That was a life-changing lesson that made my heart lighter.

I started looking at my relationship with myself, too. I was mothering and dating here and there, but I wasn't doing anything to really make myself proud since graduating high school. So, I enrolled in training to obtain my certification as a nursing assistant.

The training, which took about three months, teaches students how to care for patients in hospitals, nursing homes, or home care. The work itself is pretty routine with helping patients eat, bathe, get dressed, groom themselves, move from the bed to the wheelchair or the wheelchair to the toilet, and repositioning.

CNAs provide the basic level of care for people who cannot consistently perform these day-to-day activities on their own, usually elders. I worked with Alzheimer's patients for years before shifting to private home care where the pay is a little better.

It didn't take long to realize that being a nursing assistant wasn't going to cut it. They weren't paid much at all, even with home care. I wanted to be able to provide for my children with more than the bare minimum. Plus, living from paycheck to paycheck is mentally, emotionally, and physically exhausting.

So, I decided to go to college for nursing. I enjoyed helping people, I was patient when it came to helping those in need, and I had started learning about our bodies' natural ability to heal themselves, so I figured I'd make a wonderful nurse. I was no longer my parents' dependent, and I certainly couldn't afford college, so I signed up for a government program that would pay for my school under certain conditions, including taking a few preliminary classes. One of my first classes in the program was a self-esteem class. That was my first time even hearing that word. When I learned what it meant, I knew that I didn't have any.

I drew a giraffe with a long neck and a small head pointing down at the ground. We cracked up laughing at that picture. As hilarious as it was (and still is), that was my truth. I didn't find myself attractive in the least bit. Things that had been told to me over the years, whether as a joke or as a statement intended to hurt me, stuck with me.

I will never forget one day in class, there was an older lady who walked up to me, looked me in the eye, and said, "You have a beautiful spirit!" No one had ever said anything like that to me before. I am sure that was the beginning of my self-love journey.

My stepdad took me shopping at the mall one day when I was in high school. That moment meant so much to me. I was finally leaving the mall with bags instead of the thrift store, and I felt I'd gotten celebrity treatment there.

In the thrift stores, you're left to your own devices. In the mall, the store associate helped me find the perfect outfit and the perfect size for me. It was a white jumpsuit with a low-cut V in the back. The associate took a red scarf and tied it around my waist as a belt. I felt fabulous! Wearing it made me actually feel kind of special. Then my mom crushed my world the second time I wore it.

"You think you cute?" she asked me.

"Huh?" I answered.

"You think you're cute. You're not, You're ugly."

I crumbled inside. The small stories that I'd been telling myself of how I was kind of growing into myself and becoming kind of cute came crashing down. How dare I have the nerve to feel pretty, to feel special? "She's right," I thought. "I am ugly."

Then, of course, there were the kids at school who had their things to say about how I looked. My mind kept score of all those hurtful statements for years. Even after I grew up, started meditating, and began forgiving my parents, it still didn't erase my negative feelings about myself. I still felt unattractive, and many of my decisions, especially those pertaining to men, were based on that feeling. It wasn't until taking the self-esteem class, though, that I realized how deeply rooted my problem was.

Unfortunately, college didn't last long for me. I was trying to go to school while working full-time and raising two children. Working the third shift allowed me the time to go to school, but my focus was shot. On top of working, I was also on welfare to help me make ends meet, but it still wasn't enough. I dropped out so that I could work more hours to better support myself and my two daughters financially.

In between working and raising the kids, I was also traveling to Atlanta on my days off every other weekend to visit Chelle, who had moved up there. The drive was close to four hours, which isn't bad if you're doing it every now and then. But I was going often. That June, I decided to just move. My spirit told me to go, and I obeyed.

My CNA certification covered me all over the state of Georgia, so it wasn't hard to find work. Why settle for doing good, though, when you can do better? One of the things that attracted me to Atlanta was seeing so many Black people living so well. That was nothing like where I'd come from. Atlanta had Black doctors and lawyers, yes, but also Black politicians, business owners, and entertainers. They were living in huge houses and driving luxury cars, and I wanted a piece of the pie. So, I decided to dance on the side.

I still had a nice body after having two kids, so I figured I'd let it make me some money. I couldn't climb the pole to save my life, so I wasn't the best dancer. My saving grace was my ability to stand out. I didn't look like everyone else. I had a nice frame, wore short blonde locks, and had my own sense of style. I didn't enjoy dancing at all. I went from one club to the next one, thinking that maybe that was the problem.

Then I met a Black girl driving a Lexus who said she worked in a strip club as a waitress. This club wasn't like the others. You could tell from the outside it was rich. I told myself that I was going to start doing that instead, and I did.

Sure enough, it paid well.

Being a waitress at the club, in addition to being a CNA on the side, paid the bills and helped me take care of my daughters, but it was very short-lived. I no longer had to take my clothes off, but the environment wasn't for me. Although I was a waitress, it still felt wrong. Whenever I have to convince myself that it's okay, it's usually not.

A lot of the women who worked at the club were on drugs, drank too much, and were generally not healthy to be around. The men didn't see us as people, they viewed us as objects to which they were entitled to say and do whatever they felt like. That phase of my life had run its course.

Then one night, I lost all my money in the bathroom. It flipped out of my garter and I didn't realize it until it was too late. That was my wake-up call. I thought, *"Girl, what are you doing?"* I was still spiritual and very much fear-based in religion too at that time, and I felt like I was going straight to hell. So, after a full meltdown in the car, until I literally threw up, I quit.

I Chose to Expand

Meditation was one of the biggest blessings that I was given. Many of my most pivotal transformations started after I began closing my eyes, shutting out the world, and tuning into the divine that lived inside of me.

That's when I realized that my parents are human just like I am. I started renovating myself from the bottom to the top, from the inside out. It was also when I learned that there was nothing left in my hometown for me.

Meditation and writing were my go-to for peace. Remember, I had been journaling since I was a young girl and leaning into forgiving my parents. I started writing poetry. It was healing for me to just write whatever came up for me.

I was one of those people who loved to take care of others. It warmed my soul and gave me purpose to be a problem solver. I started smudging my home, lighting incense, and trying to truly figure out who I was and why I was here. I started questioning a lot of the beliefs that I had. For instance, why would God allow the children He loved to burn in hell? Why weren't we able to ask God questions? I felt that I was growing a personal relationship with The Most High God. I could talk to Him now like a friend.

God presents us with models for new opportunities in the form of people and places, but it's up to us to decide if we want it or not. What I wanted out of life, I knew that I couldn't achieve in my hometown.

It was scary, because I'd lived in Atlanta before, and I ended up tucking my tail and going back home. Plus, it wasn't just me this time. I had two daughters who relied on me. What if it didn't work out? The thought of moving to a new city was also exciting. What if it did work out?

People often tell me that I have a beautiful spirit. I have heard this so much that I decided to get the phrase "beautiful spirit" tattooed on my leg. I've learned since then that my spirit is my gift. Everybody has a gift. Some people are comedians. Some people are singers. Some people have a gift for design. But my spirit is my number-one gift from God. I've realized that my energy, hugs, love, and words can alter the course of someone's life. This is what God gave me that people see. That's how I ended up becoming a life coach.

I've been coaching my whole life, even as a kid. I would take people to Christ, say prayers at school, and talk to kids about their problems at home even as I was going through so much myself. Recently, I've started getting DMs from women who have gone through similar stuff as I have gone through. That's when I decided I was going to start coaching. I hate it when people say, "Everybody wants to be a life coach." Well, there are billions upon billions upon billions of people in this world, and one person can't help them all. I know that I'm doing my heart's work.

Changing people's lives is what I hope to do with this book. Otherwise, what's the use of writing it? I'm not telling this story just to be telling it. It has to change people's lives. I'm praying that other people can see themselves in my story and make changes.

An old friend reminded me that I used to say, "If God can do it for them, He can do it for me." I didn't grow up rich or privileged. My privilege was God's favor. The hardships I've been through weren't for nothing. They were for everybody who's going to be touched by this book and whose lives are going to change as a result.

By writing this book, I am living my purpose of reminding people that you can make mistakes or bad decisions and still come out like a diamond or like gold.

THE EXTRA MILE

One night, shortly after moving to Atlanta, I went to a popular nightclub called Atlanta Live. It was September 27, 1997. The club would have two separate lines to let the women in first to entice the men. Seeing all the beautiful women walk past made them even hungrier to get inside (and more willing to pay a higher door fee, too).

The club was two stories with a long spiral staircase. After walking in on the top floor through the foyer area, I noticed a guy who looked somewhat familiar standing to the left as soon as you came into the club. I walked past him and the bar to my right, straight to the glass partition, and looked over it to see how the crowd was looking. "Nice crowd," I thought to myself. I couldn't wait to dance!

While waiting on my best friend KC and my sister's boyfriend (at the time), Vince, to get inside, I decided to go stand on the wall by the familiar-looking guy, so I would be able to see when they entered the club.

I couldn't figure out where I knew him from, but his style was a conversation starter all on its own! Picture this: a slick button-up shirt with green velvet panels and sheer fabric in between, revealing his chest. "Taco meat" was on full display. He paired it perfectly with matching green velvet slacks and bone-colored shoes. Today, I would describe this look as country-dressy, but back then, his fashion sense was absolutely on point!

He looked over at me with an intimidating glare and said hi (he was giving me preacher vibes). I spoke back.

"You look really familiar to me," I said, "Like we met before or something."

"I don't think so," he answered.

"Your face looks familiar. What's your name?" I asked.

He started giving me all these aliases like Sugar Baby Lo.

"Nah, that ain't it," I said, laughing.

"They call me Carlo," he said.

"Okay, Carlo," I said back.

"What do you do?" he asked.

"I'm a nurse and I dance." I was still a CNA, but I'd stopped dancing. I just wanted to gauge his reaction when I said it. I guess my logic at the time was that I was no goodie two shoes, and I didn't need anyone in my life who was judgmental. I was new to this city, and I didn't want to be dishonest about my past. Not that I thought this guy was going to be my man, but I just felt like I could be open.

"Oh, really," he said, peering over his slanted silver metal frames with clear lenses. "Turn around. Let me see what you are workin' with." I did a cute little spin, and he seemed impressed enough. He shook his head in approval, smiled, and said, "I would love to take you to the Waffle House after this."

Today, that wouldn't offend me. Back then, I was highly offended. It felt like he was saying that all I was worth was a six-dollar breakfast in a run-down diner. That was a trigger from not feeling like I wasn't worth more than twenty dollars after my stepdad showed me the Bank of America bank statements when I was a child. My way of dealing with my self-worth issues at that time was by demanding respect and the best from men.

I felt more attractive than I did as a teenager, but I still wasn't sure if men only wanted me for one thing. I told him that I ate steak and crab legs before I left home, so I definitely didn't want to go to Waffle House. Everybody knows after a certain hour ain't nothing open but Waffle House and legs.

"Oh, I apologize," he said. "Well, I got a '65 Impala convertible, and I would love to watch the sunrise with you."

"Now you are talking," I responded. I am a Taurus, an earth sign, to the bone, so I was all about that life.

We continued our small talk until my friends walked in. As soon as they walked over, they dapped him up and said, "Hey Ceelo."

I said, "Oh, that's your name!" It still didn't sound familiar.

Ceelo knew Vince (he worked at LaFace Records as a graphic designer). Apparently, Vince had designed an album cover for his group. Vince reminded me that he had shown me that cover of him with the '65 Impala of which he spoke. I thought to myself, "That is why he initially looked familiar."

While he and Vince were talking, KC proceeded to tell me who Lo was. I told KC that he tried me by inviting me to Waffle House. He laughed and said, "Chris, he is a good guy. Very deep guy. He would probably be talking about the new world order or something." He said, "If it were any other rapper, I would tell you, 'No,' but if you decide you want to go grab a bite with him, I think it would be okay.

In my past, I was a sexually active teenager and a dancer, but it didn't matter because I still had heavy morals and a fear of God. I was raised in the church, and it was extremely tough trying to survive as a single mother and not disappoint God by doing it. I never desired to get married as some young girls dreamed, but I had no idea I was already a wife.

When I walked back over to Ceelo, he told me, "If you change your mind and decide you want to, meet me here at 2 a.m., and we can leave." I nonchalantly agreed so as not to seem desperate.

My spirit felt at peace about leaving with Ceelo after speaking to the guys about him. I went downstairs and danced my little heart out and had a couple of cocktails. I had such a good time that I ended up losing track of time.

By the time I looked at my watch, it was fifteen minutes past the time Ceelo told me to meet him back upstairs. I took off like Cinderella for the staircase. I got to about the third step from the top and slowed down to catch my cool. Again, I didn't want to seem desperate. He was still standing there, and I was beyond happy on the inside.

"You still here?" I asked him, as if I hadn't just run and prayed to God that he was.

"You ready?" he asked.

I nodded and we headed outside. Lo and behold, there wasn't a convertible in sight. Instead, he walked me to his Acura Legend, and it looked like thieves had ransacked it. Stuff was everywhere. Your car and your room are a reflection of how you're maintaining your mental health. Is it cluttered or clear? I didn't put two and two together at the time, however.

I grabbed a plastic grocery store bag off the floor and started putting mail and other random papers in it. Unconsciously, I'd already started trying to "fix" him. I also asked him what happened to the '65 convertible, and he said that he hadn't driven it that night. I asked him where we were going, and he said a spot called R. Thomas. I'd never heard of it, but he said the food was really good, so I was down.

I was later reminded that neither the club nor the album cover was my first time seeing him. Back in Charlotte, I loved thrifting. I used to dress in vintage clothes and leisure suits. That's right, butterfly collars and platform shoes. I lived inside of an old mill building that had been renovated into loft apartments.

One day, my neighbor called me and asked me to hurry and run down to her place to see something on TV. She rushed me through the door of her apartment, and as I got there, she said, "Your husband is on TV. He got the butterfly collar just like you be wearing." We laughed so hard about that back then. Turns out, she was speaking the truth and didn't even know it. It was the Goodie Mob "Soul Food" video.

"I'ma go with you, but I don't want to talk about no stars and quasars, aliens, and shit. Not tonight. I've been drinking, and I don't feel like delving that deep. We can get deep another night," I told him. We still laugh about that 'til this day.

R. Thomas is a late-night eclectic restaurant out in Buckhead. It is a tent inside and has birds in cages and flowers everywhere, and the food is delicious and fresh. We had such a good time together, and I actually appreciated seeing him talking, smacking, and licking his fingers while eating his wings. He didn't give a damn, and I liked that. He was down to earth. Then a couple walked over to the table and the dude said, "Ceelo, hey man. I hate to bother you, man, but I could not see you in person and not let you know your music saved my life."

That made me sit up. *Who am I with?* Since I was a child, my heart's work has been serving God and helping people. That man's comment let me know that there was much more to Ceelo than the dude who'd asked me to turn around so he could see my shape in the club and who'd invited me to the Waffle House. Of course, he's still a man, but that let me know there were a lot more layers to him. I made a mental note to buy some of his music and see what he was talking about for myself.

"Where you live again?" he asked me.

"Right up the street, right off Clairmont."

"I think I know where Clairmont is, but I don't necessarily know if I do. I've had a drink and I would hate to get lost driving around. If you don't mind, I could take you to my house. I have a guest room you can sleep in, and I will take you home in the morning. That way I can make sure we both are safe."

I knew he was lying. I shook my head, and he raised his hands to plead his case. I still thought he was full of it, but between enjoying his company and KC saying he was safe, I agreed. On the way to his house, he played Portishead and Black Sabbath, a rock band, which showed me that his taste in music wasn't hip hop only.

Even then, I thought he was trying to impress me. My hair was blonde, and I wasn't dressed like the average woman at that time, so I figured he was trying to woo me on the way to his home. Turns out, he appreciates a wide range of music. It's just who he is. And if he was making an assumption about me, he was right. Back then, I listened to Alanis Morissette, No Doubt, and shit like that. I loved it.

His home was so nicely decorated that I just knew a woman had something to do with it. Being the other woman just ain't my cup of tea. I've always said I never want to be the face behind another woman's pain because I know how that feels. That wasn't the case, though. He's just what some would call a metrosexual, a man who's interested in shopping, fashion, décor, and aesthetics.

We sat in his formal living room, and he shared so much with me about his life growing up. He talked about how he was put in special classes because they perceived him as slow, but he really is a genius. I could tell that from our conversations. He told me ideas he had created for other artists like Usher.

I remember asking him why he felt so comfortable sharing so much with me. I told him he had to be careful about whom he divulges his ideas to because everyone isn't so honest. He said, "I don't know what it is, I feel like I can trust you." He was right. I wouldn't have shared the things he told me with anyone.

After hours of talking, he took me by hand and showed me to his room. The first song he played was "I'd Die Without You," a song by P.M. Dawn from the *Boomerang* soundtrack. He didn't know it, but *Boomerang* is one of my favorite movies (that and *Pretty Woman*). He successfully wooed me because I was all in. I undressed, and he asked if he could take a picture of me wearing a Goodie Mob shirt with no bottoms. "I want to put it over my bed," he said.

"Hell no, I'm not like that. I only agreed to come here because my friend said you were safe," I snapped. He almost ruined the moment, but between the liquor and the lust, I was still down. I was grown and could do what I wanted, when I wanted, and with whomever I wanted.

He said, "I want to turn the lights on."

I thought, *"Wow, he is confident in himself."* That turned me on, too. The sun rose, I sobered up, and my perspective on what had happened completely changed. I felt so stupid. I let a rapper have sex with me the first night I met him. *He probably thinks I do this all the time.*

True to his word, he said he was taking me home. The whole ride home, I told myself if he didn't ask me for my number or ask how he could stay in touch with me, I would feel even more stupid. It wasn't supposed to turn out like that.

I told my friend KC what happened, and he stopped talking to me for almost two weeks. "I told you he was safe to go eat with, not sleep with. This man gonna put you in a song. I don't want people looking at you like that because that's not who you are."

My thought was, "Obviously that is who I am because I did it." I didn't consider myself promiscuous, but I also didn't want people to categorize me as a Puritan because I wasn't that, either. So, although I was beating myself up on the inside, on the outside I played it cool—later on with KC and on the ride home with Lo.

I didn't apologize or try to explain that last night's behavior was out of my character. I just quietly hoped he asked me for my number because I really did enjoy his company and I felt safe with him.

We pulled up to Chelle's apartment complex, where I was staying, and the moment of truth slapped itself on the dashboard. Was he going to ask me for my number or not? He didn't ask the entire drive over, so I assumed it wasn't going to happen.

I turned to get out of the car, and he asked. "Do you mind if I get your number?" I wrote it down, and he said he'd call me. I didn't get his number, so I waited and waited. Turns out, he lost it. He remembered Vince, though, and went to LaFace and asked him for my number. He called me and explained what happened, and I was impressed. He could've easily shrugged it off when he lost the number, but he went the extra mile, literally, to stay in contact with me.

The second or third time he called me, I remember it being very late at night. I told him that when I answered but with a little more attitude. "It's late. Don't be booty calling me."

He tried to clarify, "No, no, it's not like that."

I was already on a roll. "I just put my kids to bed, and they're on a regimen.

You have kids, he asked. Yes, two girls. They have to be in bed by nine. Don't get it twisted because you got lucky that one time."

The following year, he proved KC right. Ceelo did talk about me in a song, but it was with the utmost respect.

This is Carlito from a couple of days ago. You sound tired.

Forgive me if I've called you too late.

But what better time to relate mind-state?

Where could I begin?

Has anyone ever told you, you got beautiful skin?

I Chose Boundaries

Why aren't we taught about boundaries early on in life? Maybe because a lot of adults don't know how to set them.

Setting boundaries could save your life. I know it could have kept me from some really bad heartaches. Only we know our pain tolerances, what we can deal with, and what our deal breakers are. We will set ourselves on fire to keep others warm but not realize we are allowing our own demise.

It is perfectly fine to say no, but when you are a people pleaser because you want to be loved, you are willing to betray yourself by allowing behaviors or doing things that you know you don't want to do.

If you can just get the recognition of being the best daughter, friend, cousin, aunt, sister, girlfriend, etc., then you feel like sacrificing yourself is worth it. Just to feel sometimes a false sense of love and care is just the crumbs you need to survive.

You know self-betrayal is not truly loving yourself. In fact, it is the complete opposite. When you love yourself, you don't do things to let yourself down, and you don't allow others to hurt and disrespect you.

Consider yourself a priority because you truly are. Why is everyone else worthy of your time, energy, love, and respect, but you? The way we will wear ourselves out to take care of everyone and leave ourselves for last is senseless.

It is so unfair to us when we do that. If you weren't here, how would everyone get along? They would figure it out. The thought of you not being with your loved ones is quite upsetting, but unfortunately so many have left this earth earlier considering others and placing themselves last.

You might think that your job and satisfying your boss are of utmost importance. Yet, when you are out of commission for whatever reason, they can easily let you go. Your health and getting yearly physicals are put on the back burner because you are too busy taking care of others. By the time some of us find out we are ill, it is too late. You are there for everyone financially, but when you are in need, there is no one for you to turn to.

There is absolutely nothing wrong with excelling in your workplace, physically taking care of others, and loving others, but please take care of yourself first. How will you get everything on your to-do list done if you are ill, depressed, or God forbid, not here?

I was thirty-six when I was diagnosed with Graves' disease. I had a partial hysterectomy and one surgery per year for three years. I've also dealt with heart issues. Since then, some of the most important lessons I have learned are balance and saying no. You never want to be in a situation where you are giving everything and are left with nothing.

You don't get a prize at the end of giving everything away. You don't get an Oscar because you gave the most away this year. You don't get shit. If anything, you get depleted. Then you have nothing else for yourself, and it's not fair to you. Put yourself first, and then you take care of everybody else. As long as you're the one who gives, people are going to take. You have to set boundaries, and you don't owe anyone any explanations.

My health issues have also taught me that I truly don't have control over my next breath. Everything can change in a second. So why not do beautiful things in life with the things that you do have control over? Why not eat right? Why not exercise? Why not speak positively?

Your life truly matters.

HIS PERFECT IMPERFECTIONS

"Chris, I want you to be my main lady," Lo told me one day. We'd been seeing each other for about six or seven months, so it was time. That's the longest I'd ever waited to shift from dating to being in a relationship, but I appreciated that time. It allowed us to get to know each other.

During this seven-month period, I fell head over heels in love with Lo. He was extremely funny and honest, and he made me feel safe and loved. We spent the bulk of our time in the beginning at his home watching funny movies, and TV shows like SouthPark, cooking, and making love.

He could cook two things very well: turkey burgers and wings. It was a treat to have. What I didn't appreciate, however, was being called his "main lady." That suggested that I was the lead in the choir. If I was going to be with him, then it needed to only be me.

"Your main lady? How many others?" I asked.

"No, no, no. I just want to be with you. You'll be my girl?"

Of course, I said yes. I loved that man. I also understand how major that moment was for him. First of all, I was his first real girlfriend. He'd dated someone in high school and she'd broken his heart, and he decided that women weren't trustworthy from that point forward.

Second, he didn't want to date women with children. He figured if he'd waited and didn't have any, then he should be with a woman who made the same choice. So, this was new stomping grounds all around.

Third, people loved Goodie Mob but they *loved* Ceelo. These were young, fly entertainers whose music was played all over the world but most definitely in their hometown of Atlanta, Georgia. So, you can only imagine how many women wanted to get close to him.

He wanted to be with me, though. As grateful as I was that he asked me for my number that morning he dropped me off after our first night together, I was even more elated that he wanted me to be his woman.

Making Space

I cared for him, and I showed it in every language of love out there, especially acts of service. I cooked, cleaned, and just cared about his well-being. I wasn't doing it to be manipulative or desperate. If I'm close to someone and see a way that I can help them, I do it. I don't even think about it.

Lo's guest room was piled so high with clothes that you couldn't see the bed or the floor. His time was limited with touring, so he wasn't washing his clothes, he'd just buy more. I cleaned it, and I remember he joked that he'd forgotten there was even a bed in there.

My friend KC got annoyed with me after learning that I was washing Lo's clothes at the laundromat. "You just met him, Chris. You always do that. That's who you are, I understand that, but you gon' have to learn how to slow down." I knew exactly what KC was saying and what he was trying to protect me from.

"But he ain't got nobody to help him," I'd say. If I felt taken advantage of, then that would be something else, but I didn't. I felt like he made my life easier and that was a way to reciprocate.

He'd always say, "I fell in love with you because you took initiative. Nobody had ever done that in my life."

Another thing is that I didn't try to hold Lo to expectations that were designated for an exclusive couple before we became that. I cared about him, but I wasn't crazy. I know that he was seeing other women. That was fine with me because I wasn't his woman. I just demanded respect.

For instance, after about the second time of seeing condoms in his trash can when I came over, I put my foot down. "If I come over and see something like this one more time, I'm not coming back. Take out the trash and wash the sheets. Have some respect for me."

I couldn't believe that the women he was used to dealing with did nothing for him and didn't check him about anything. You can tell how a man feels about himself in the choices he makes with women.

When Lo finally asked me to be his woman, that's also when we decided that it was time for him to meet my daughters. I was very protective of them and refused to have men in and out of their lives. Whoever I'm dating is not their "uncle," and they do not need to know all of their mother's "friends." I'd long ago decided that any man who met my children was going to be in a serious situation.

He was on the same page too, though, because he didn't want to risk falling in love with my kids and then not being able to see them anymore if we ended things. That was right up my alley, so I was cool with it.

We took the kids to Piccadilly at Greenbrier, a cafeteria-style restaurant that serves typical Southern foods like fried chicken, macaroni, green beans, mashed potatoes, rice, and gravy. Lo loved Piccadilly back then. We grabbed our trays, went through the line, got our food, and sat at the table.

I remember he looked at my oldest daughter and whispered across the table to me, "Sierra looks just like me." He grabbed his chest like he couldn't believe it. She really does. Throughout our entire relationship, and even today, no one questions that he's her father because they look alike.

At that point, he just knew that it was meant to be. He loved and still loves those girls. He even gave them nicknames. One was Smiley, and the other was Rabbit.

From that point forward, we were a family. He wanted more kids, eight total. "That ain't happening," I'd say, "Not even including the two I already have."

He wanted a son first then some girls. We'd stay up late in bed talking about all kinds of things. That was one of our favorite things to do. One time we stayed up all night coming up with kids' names—Moody Blue, Silky Red, and Cleva.

We told Erykah Badu that we almost named our son Cleva, she laughed and asked us to change his name. This particular part of the song mirrored us so perfectly:

My dress ain't cost nothin' but seven dollars

But I made it fly

And I'll tell ya why

'Cause I'm cleva

When I bust a rhyme

I'm cleva

Always on ya' mind

She's cleva

And I really wanna grow

But why come

I'm the last to know?[3]

Making a Life

Not too long after getting serious, we started living together. He still had the house he owned, but the air quality was so bad that he ended up in the hospital one time with an asthma attack. That was our first big serious thing. He could barely breathe.

The first time I saw his asthma pump, I questioned why he smoked. Chelle had really bad asthma growing up, so I was used to it. Thankfully he survived because it scared me so bad.

That night at the hospital ended up becoming a running joke in Atlanta. I'd climbed in the little gurney with him, and a nurse walked in and was like "Ma'am, you got to get out the bed!" So, people joked from that day on that Lo tried to get some in the hospital.

After that, he stayed at my apartment with me and the girls. That's where he started doing production. He brought his keyboard with the beat machine on it and started making beats. I had two royal blue dope-ass vintage sofas that sat on the floor with silver legs wrapped around them. He'd sit the machine on it and go to work.

In December of '99, we found a house that we loved and filled out the paperwork for it. I was so excited. I thought, *"Oh my God, I'm gonna get my first house with the person I'm in love with. He got some shit with him, but I'ma love him through it. We gon' figure this out. He's gonna be the best husband in the world one day, and I'm going to be his wife. This my man for the rest of my life."*

We weren't approved for the house just yet, but simply finding one that we both loved felt amazing. It would've been nice to get married before the house, but I was fine with getting the house first. As long as at least one of the two came before the baby carriage, I was fine. Then, as fate would have it, I found out I was pregnant.

We'd had a little argument and swore we were done with each other. He went to the studio, and I was at the house. My stomach started feeling sick, and I threw up. I'm not a sickly person at all. In fact, he told me one day, "I never heard you even cough before. You might be the healthiest woman I have ever met."

So, when I started throwing up, I knew I was pregnant. We hadn't done anything at all to prevent pregnancy. Despite already having two children, I assumed I was sterile. He'd get upset when my monthly came on because he wanted kids so bad. I'd cry because if not having children was a deal breaker for him, then it was bound to end because my period came faithfully every month. I never even considered if maybe it was him who couldn't have children.

I called him and told him that I just threw up. He was probably like "Girl, we mad at each other right now. You just trying to find a reason to call me." I reminded Lo that I hadn't had anything to drink for weeks and that I never get sick. "Grab a pregnancy test on your way home."

He was still a little cynical and kept asking me if I was for real. He must've told them at the studio that he immediately had to go because he never got home so fast. I went to the bathroom to take the EPT, then sat it on our master bathroom counter. The timer went off, and I told him to go check the results. When he looked back at me, he looked five years old in the face.

He shook his head yes.

"What are you talking about?" I asked him.

"You are pregnant, Chris."

Although I knew it, I couldn't believe it. I knew before I even took the test that I was pregnant, but I still could not wrap my brain around the fact that I was with child. I laughed and cried at the same damn time. I was happy that I wasn't sterile. I was happy that he was so happy. I knew how much he wanted to be a father. And I knew this would bring us closer together.

They were tears of joy, but there was some disappointment swimming around in them. We'd found a house, but it wasn't ours yet. We weren't even married, and I already had two children with two different men. Nonetheless, I was ecstatic, hence the simultaneous boo-hoo crying and hysterical laughter.

While he called his grandmother, who was absolutely thrilled, I reflected on the night we conceived. A few days before that, we'd gotten into it, and I put him out. I packed all of his stuff into garbage bags and told him he had to go. He might've left that night, but he didn't move out. When he came back, I smelled another woman on him. Not literally, but it was like I could feel the energy or presence of a woman.

He cried and apologized profusely before even answering if he had been with someone else. We ended up making love in the dark on the bathroom floor. I saw these dark figures in the air that appeared darker than the darkness. They were very calming spirits though. It didn't scare me at all. I was mesmerized. That was the day that we conceived. It was a gift.

His phone rang, and it was his sister, who was also our realtor. He said, "Shedonna, we're having a baby!" She was like "What?!" He said, "Yeah, we just took the test. We just found out. I was about to call you." Her next response took us to the moon. "I was calling y'all to say you got the house." The same day we found out we were having a baby, we also found out we were getting our first house together.

It felt like everything was coming together. Whatever we'd been arguing about in the past didn't even matter anymore. Our future was bright, and I was ready for it. We felt like we were on top of the world.

Making Promises

Something was still missing though: our vows. I hated the thought of going to the doctor and being treated as inferior because I was a young Black woman with three children, three baby daddies, and no husband. More importantly, I needed that confirmation that he wasn't going anywhere, that he was really in this with me.

Regardless of how much I wanted to get married, I would never push a man to marry me. I expressed that I wasn't happy bringing another child into the world as a girlfriend, but I also stressed that if he wasn't ready, then I didn't want him to do it. I said, "Don't marry me because I'm pregnant or because you feel pressured by people to do it. Marry me because I'm the woman you want to spend the rest of your life with. If it ain't that, then keep it."

One day, while in my apartment (our house was still under construction), I was sitting on the bed, and he knelt down on one knee on the floor beside me. "What are you doing? Why you over here?" I asked him, being silly.

"Chris, I want you to be my wife. Will you marry me?"

"Stop playing. Don't play like that!" He didn't have a ring, so he couldn't be for real. I playfully slapped his arm. He didn't budge. I looked at his face and realized he wasn't playing.

"I'm serious. I want you to be my wife. It ain't nobody else I want to be with. We 'bout to get this house. Now you 'bout to give me a baby. I want you to be my wife."

"Hell yeah, I'll marry you!"

In February 2000, I proposed that we just get married at the courthouse and then have a wedding after I had the baby, but he wasn't having it.

He said, "Chris, I'm not marrying you in no courthouse. We gonna have a wedding." He allowed me to pick out my diamond and helped me design my own ring. It was a stunning floating diamond.

We planned the wedding in thirty days and married on March 18, 2000, at his grandmother's church with all of our loved ones. We were broke as hell. His family, including his aunts and sister, organized the entire event. Lil G from Silk graciously sang for free, while DJ Romeo Cologne, a fan of Lo's, volunteered his DJ services. The preacher only requested a small donation, and we gave him around $100. A talented soul named Shenelle created my wedding dress, and long tube tops with pants for my bridesmaids, all in white. I provided the fabric, and she made the outfits without charge. L.A. Reid generously covered the cost of our reception.

Originally, I envisioned a small, intimate wedding with about 75 guests. However, once we began inviting family, LaFace Records colleagues, and friends, the guest list expanded to over 200! At the ceremony, Lo serenaded me, and there wasn't a dry eye in the room. The reception was stunning; he arranged for a spotlight to shine directly on me from the balcony, he wanted all eyes on his bride.

Making Moves

Shortly after we got married, Lo was headed on tour with the group. The day he was leaving to fly to Japan, I could tell he wasn't settled in his spirit. We said our goodbyes and he left.

I'm not sure if he was gone for two hours. I remember hearing the door. He walked into the bedroom and said, "I can't do it, Chris. I quit the group." I was shocked. He said, "I was sitting on the plane and the pilot said they were de-icing the wings, and something told me to get off the plane. I gotta go solo."

When you are in a relationship and your significant other is so solid in a decision and you trust them, you support them. If he had said he was going to stop doing music to open a donut shop, I would have supported him.

I was scared and excited for him at the same time. It wasn't about the guys; he had liberated himself. Just like Mary "Squeak" Agnes from The Color Purple, he wanted to sing. He didn't want to rap anymore, he wanted to use one of his other gifts. As a family man, the head of a growing household, he wanted to move differently.

The idea for Goodie Mob to branch out and do their own thing as individuals had already been planted. I was on the tour bus the day they decided to do it. The *World Party* album was released on December 21, 1999. T-Mo suggested that they all go solo after the album. Lo agreed. When he decided to actually cut ties, the group wasn't happy at all.

As great of a rapper as Lo was, he wanted to sing. That's where his heart was. Being in the group made him good money. He made money from the albums, but the real money came from the shows. Once he went solo, there weren't any shows initially. There wasn't even a record deal.

Ordinarily, I would've just worked it out on the job and carried us until he got back on his feet, but I couldn't — I was on bed rest. I worked almost the entire pregnancy, then I got into a car accident where I was hit in the back. I started spotting after that, so my doctor put me on bed rest.

There was nothing I could do to help the situation but do my best to keep him encouraged. He called Busta Rhymes, who'd left Leaders of the New School and did his first solo project in 1996. Busta said that going solo was inevitable.

He told Lauryn Hill what he really wanted to do and she said, "Sing." Quoting Lauryn, "It could all be so simple," and it was, but it wasn't. It's never easy on a man when he isn't providing for his family like he wants to. He'd take small projects here and there, mainly from street dudes who were making music. They'd pay him between $5,000 to $10,000 for a feature, but it was hardly enough to relax.

We had hardly any money. That's hard for some people to believe because you see a person on TV and think that because they're famous, they're also rich, but those are two different things. Wealth is totally different from riches. He was wealthy in every way but the cash. He had good health, a loving family, and a strong support system, and he was doing what he loved to do, but he didn't have the money. All our needs were always met, though, by the grace of God.

We closed on the house on a Friday, got married on a Saturday, and started moving in on Sunday. My nerves got to me at times, but overall, my faith held me down. I knew we'd be okay. Lo came to bed one night, not long after we got married. He told me that he cried out to God on his knees while in the shower.

I told him that I had such peace about things and reminded him that we'd be okay. "You prayed. Now surrender," I told him.

We woke up to a phone call the next morning from Goodie Mob's old management office. Lo was one of the contributors to Carlos Santana's album, *Supernatural*. He and Lauryn Hill provided lead vocals on a track called "Do You Like the Way."

The manager put Lo down for a penny or so on every CD sold on that album. From that, Lo had a check for six figures. It was the most money he had ever made from music.

Goodie Mob didn't get a good deal from the jump, and they had to split it four ways after paying management. So, this was major on so many levels. The checks kept coming, and he kept working on his solo project, *Cee-Lo Green and His Perfect Imperfections*, which was released in April of 2002.

The song "Getting' Grown" from the album was Lo's first Grammy nomination in the Best Urban/Alternative Performance category. He didn't win it, but the nomination was a key indicator that he was headed down the right track.

Financially, we were good after that initial check from Santana's album. The adversary walked in with the money though, because, as we all know, money makes you more of who you already are.

Making a Break for It

To this day, I have no doubt that my husband loved me deeply. He demonstrated his love through beautiful gestures and actions. Although we got married as adults, he was still on his journey to becoming a man. He tried his best to fulfill his roles as a husband and father, but he lacked guidance — his father passed away when he was two and he had no examples of successful marriages around him.

I was madly in love with my husband. He saw greatness in me, perhaps even more than I saw in myself at the time. Beautiful surprises were a regular occurrence in our home. Coming off tour, he would present me with new suitcases full of the most stunning things he had picked out for me. He would lay an outfit on the bed for me to put on and surprise me with a limo to take us to dinner, just because.

When we were dating, he would send me flowers with cards reading, "Here I go loving you again." It made me feel like that's who he truly was. He could have been enjoying his twenties living a rock and roll lifestyle, yet he chose me.

I also witnessed his kindness in how he treated others. He had a compassionate heart. I remember one particular day at the Cub Foods grocery store encountered a struggling family (parents and their children). It became apparent to us that they were low on funds and were trying to figure out what they could afford to buy for dinner that night. The kids recognized him and approached him for an autograph. He gladly signed it and then discreetly gave them money. He told them to treat their parents to dinner. When he returned to the car, I saw tears quietly streaming down his face. I remember being so moved by his generosity.

I believe his childhood traumas, old pain, resentments, and unforgiveness were hard to shake, so he took his frustrations out on the closest person to him — he didn't have the tools to place his anger in the right place. Anger is a natural emotion that we all have felt. We have to know how to approach those feelings and deal with them or they can keep you in bondage or even land you in jail.

As our marriage neared its end, there was no room for error. We were easily irritated with one another. Over time, each negative episode eroded the love and admiration I once felt for my husband.

There were numerous instances of abuse, with verbal abuse sometimes being more hurtful than physical. I distinctly recall one occasion when he cursed at me up close, and I could feel his spit in my earlobe. It was a deeply humiliating and soul-crushing moment. He screamed, "I hate you; you hear me? I am not apologizing for it tomorrow because I mean what I'm saying, I hate you. You're a fucked-up mother, a fucked-up wife, a fucked-up person, and I hate you."

You take someone's last name, believing they will be your protector, only to find they're the one you fear. I grew weary of the frequent episodes where his demeanor resembled that of Chucky. I realize now it must have been difficult for him to navigate what I considered rules and regulations in our marriage, which he viewed as limitations.

I was a full-time interior designer, and I remember getting off of work and sitting in my car for a while and not wanting to go inside. I had promised myself years ago after seeing one of my dear friends in an abusive relationship that if I was ever afraid or uncomfortable to go into my own home, I would end it. So, I knew it was over, but I was just trying to figure out how to get out.

Things had been rocky with the label, and it ended up shutting down. That means that he ended up getting dropped. All I kept thinking about was that he was going to take it out on me.

The night that they told him that the label was shutting down, we were in New York. When we went back to the hotel room, he lost his temper again. I fled from our room to my friend's hotel room barefoot. The next day, there was another apology, but I knew that the behavior would not change.

When we got back to Atlanta, there was a show that night. I got dressed up and put on my invisible mask to pretend that I was happy. There was a guy in the club who said to Lo, "You with Beyonce, ain't you?" I assumed it was because of the way that I was dressed and wore my hair. I had on a patent leather outfit, and my hair was a mix of blonde and curly individual braids.

My husband lost his cool with the guy because he complimented me. When we got back in the limo, Lo told his manager what the guy said, and he agreed with the guy. I could tell that Lo got even more upset. On the ride home, he started cursing, yelling, and pushing the side of my temple with his fingers. I remember seeing a police officer parked on the side of the road, and he told me if I stopped, he was going to kill me that night. I had already had a sense that that was going to happen anyway.

The rest of the ride home I was trying to figure out how I was going to get away. When we pulled up to the house, I opened the garage. I stalled by going to get my purse out of the trunk.

He was unlocking the garage door and walking into the house, so I ran, jumped into the car, put it in reverse, sped out of our driveway, and called my mom. When my mom picked up the phone, I was confused because I could tell she was out, but she was babysitting the children that night so why wouldn't she be home?

She didn't say hello. She said, "Where are you? I've been to your house twice!" She told me not to go back home. She said she was asleep and she could hear me screaming that my husband was going to kill me. She said God told her to get on her knees and pray for me, and she did. She said she left the kids at her house, put the alarm on, and prayed that they would not get up and set it off, but she needed to come check on me. She said, "Please do not go back home."

I said, "I'm not. I'm on my way to your house." I don't think that it would've been his intention to kill me, but I do believe in divine intervention. That night, the strangling may have gone too far, but it was the confirmation that I needed that it was time to end this chapter of my life.

The next day I filed for divorce. This was my second time filing for divorce, but this was my first time accepting that I couldn't go back.

The next morning, I called his sister and her husband to tell them that it was over. He called me and asked me when I was going to bring his car back. I told him that the children had school and needed to come home, so he needed to find somewhere else to go and that I was filing for divorce.

I've been through so many things in my life, but divorce was one of the hardest things I've ever endured. Have you ever tried to leave someone that you were madly in love with?

I had no money when I left. I actually had to return an expensive gift to the Gucci store to pay my attorney fees. My peace, respect, and self-worth are priceless. So, I left with nothing monetary.

I fell into depression and wouldn't eat, couldn't sleep or bathe. It lasted about two weeks. One morning, I got a letter slid under my door from my daughter Sierra. She let me know that I was loved and asked me to please get up, get dressed, and go out and do something nice for myself. That letter confirmed for me that I needed to get up and get on with life.

I did move on, but for years afterward, we continued living pretty much the same way. Although we were divorced, we lived as if we were still married in separate homes.

I Chose to Stay

Hurt people hurt people. That's one of the realest statements ever said. It's not a point-blank-period situation though. Hurt people who haven't dealt with their hurt are the ones who hurt people. That was the case for many of the men I attracted in my life, including my father, stepdad, a few of my ex-boyfriends, and my ex-husband.

Too many of our men were never given the space or the permission to be afraid, angry, or sad. So, they bottle the emotions up until they explode. It might be every now and then for some or more often than not for others. Find somebody who feels powerless over a situation and angry about it, and I can almost guarantee they'll find someone to flex what power they do have over them.

The first time I saw Lo get upset was on the tour bus. Someone was playing with a toy laser, and it set him off. Once he identified the culprit, he stormed over to him and it took me and a few other people to calm him down. Personally, I was terrified because we didn't even know if it was a real gun or not yet. I looked past it, more grateful that it wasn't real and that a throwdown didn't take place.

Slowly but surely, his anger turned towards me. I remember going to a concert with him one night and a woman approached me and referred to me as his "new hoe." Offended ain't the word. I felt so disrespected! Instead of using the wine glass I had in my hand and going upside her head like I really wanted to, I told Lo that I was going to the bar and for him to handle it.

While getting my drink, I ran into his jeweler. He spoke and, not wanting to be rude, I stopped to speak. Lo interrupted the conversation and asked me about it, but what he was really upset about was the fact that I walked away from the woman instead of putting her in her place.

We went back and forth about it and got in the car, and he was still seething. He punched the vents in the car and busted up the whole dashboard. That was my first time being afraid of him. We weren't living together just yet, so I remember grabbing my house keys and getting ready to jump out of the car.

As soon as the car slowed down, I got out and took off running. He was right on my tail. His close friend was with us and tried to stop him to no avail. Was this really happening? His hands were around my throat. The man that I had fallen in love with was strangling me. I don't know what stopped him.

The next day, I had to wear a white button-up shirt to hide the bruises on my neck, although the bruises on my heart were the ones that stuck with me for years and years. Lo was in so much pain. I thought I could love him through all of it. I'm not sure why people hurt the people that are the closest to them. Maybe it is because they think that no matter what, they won't leave them.

I cut him off after that—or at least I tried to. His cousin worked with me at the time and asked me not to break up with him. He said that Lo had never had a real girlfriend before, so all of this was new to him, but he'd never do it again.

I stayed away for a short time but then he went to see a counselor. I swore I wouldn't take him back, but I did. Again, and again and again. The details of every incident and every story aren't necessary to share. Yet, I do realize that I betrayed myself by staying when the behavior had not changed.

From the little girl Christina's perspective, I think she was still looking for punishment for not being enough and not feeling worthy. It was so confusing to feel like your knight in shining armor, the one who does the sweetest and most magical things for you is also the person you are afraid of.

My Rebirth

Mother Zen Speaks

I am so very sorry, Christina.

I know that you are here on this plane and all of the things that were happening to you were so painful and scary. I have relived them over and over, and I'm apologizing because I feel like your spirit knew you were coming here to have these experiences. That's why you were so excited to be here. Yet, your human side had no idea how those experiences would knock the wind out of you time and time again.

You are perfect in God's sight. I want you to know that I am so proud of you for bringing us this far. You no longer have to betray yourself or sabotage the good things or people that you're blessed with. I beg of you to forgive yourself. You were a child, so how could a child be at fault? You deserve the same grace that you've given to many. You deserve forgiveness, love, and understanding.

Thank you for coming forward and always protecting us, especially during traumas. I appreciate you loving people the way that you do. I honor the fact that you have forgiven everyone who has wronged you in any way, and I'm proud that you have let go of the guilt that you carried for the way you may have hurt other people. All hurt people know is hurt. That's why they end up hurting others. What has been a protective mechanism for us has also caused other people pain. I pray that they have forgiven us, but, if they haven't, I pray that you forgive yourself, regardless.

You know from the depths of your soul that you were trying to protect yourself, not to hurt anyone else. The Most High God knows that too. Now I need you to let go of all the pain and continue staying in a place of humility and love. You are a spirit having a powerful human experience.

Going forward, your next chapter will be your best chapter. You no longer have to jump up to try to save and protect me. You can release all anxieties, fear, and panic.

You can rest, little girl, I have us. I am a decorated warrior now, a Queen Mother, an adult. I can forgive and have the adult conversations. I can walk it out and talk it out. I never have to get quiet or revisit the bubble for any reason.

We are doing wonderfully!

We are loved and we are love! Keep going!

Mother Zen

I Chose to Leave

Ten years to the day that Lo and I met, my first home purchase sale took place. As a self-employed divorced mother of three, this was a dream deferred. Lo's sister DeeDee was our real estate agent. Yes, I said, "our" because at this point in my life, I still looked at things like it was an "us." Shedonna took us around to see quite a few houses.

I remember driving up to a house and the yard wasn't kept, but I saw two porches—one on the top floor and one on the bottom. We parked at the bottom of the driveway and on the street. As we walked up, I looked at this house and felt this was the one. It was built solid in 1987 and rebuilt in 1991. It came with a fireplace and a brick oven. I decided on this house the moment we stepped foot into it. It was bank-owned, and we put an offer on it.

Again, Lo was right there for me, helping me look for the perfect home, and he put a large down payment on the house. I appreciated it so very much. It was the first time I had a home in my name based on my finances as an interior designer.

I was so ecstatic because owning my own home was a dream of mine since I was a child. The first home where I was on the deed was exciting, but my life had now gone in a different direction. Now as a divorcée, I had to start all over again with a new life. It was basically just my address that changed because although my physical body left, my heart stayed with him.

Here we were in 2007, three years separated, two years officially divorced, and we were still doing a lot of the things the same, meaning spending holidays and birthdays together and still being intimate. It didn't matter to me about there being others because I never saw or heard about anyone else. I also had some love affairs in between.

When we aren't loving ourselves or being true to ourselves, we aren't at ease, and that is when disease creeps in. There is a saying that goes "Self-love is when you aren't doing things to betray yourself." I created disease in my body because of my mind, anger, and resentment. Lo, called this new home "the sick house" because I got really sick in this home.

I was so certain after my divorce that my ex-husband was going to get himself healed and return home. It was so difficult to release the relationship because we were still intimate and did things the same for so long. The sex, the conversations, the flirting, and the accommodating were confusing. So, I pictured myself waiting on him until he returned.

One weekend after being flown out by Lo on a private plane to Los Angeles, I was belittled in front of our son. That was the last straw. After a gut-wrenching dinner, we were in the streets of LA arguing while our son was in the car. The level of disrespect was enough to never speak to this soul ever again. "Country bitch, you will never be half the woman she is," now has no bearing over me, but during that time, it broke my heart. All of that happened because I didn't want his new woman to come have dinner with us, since I didn't know much about her.

Many times, over, I should have walked away from him and never looked back. Aside from my love for him, the reason I didn't was because I was trying to protect our blended family. That night when his woman pulled up, I was distraught, and I told her everything I could think of.

A few nights before Lo had asked me to spend the night with him, something in my soul told me to refuse. I had just found out about her at his grandma's funeral. I didn't know that they lived together in L.A. I felt bamboozled and used. Lo had purchased me two beautiful cars and a high-end condo for me with cash, and we were still being intimate, so I felt blindsided.

Before that night, I was still with him off and on throughout their relationship unknowingly. I was on the streets with my heart ripped out of my chest. I cried the five-hour flight back to Atlanta, and for the next few days.

Lo called me to apologize for not being honest about what was going on with him and his relationship. This was right before the holidays, so he asked me if they could come to Christmas dinner. I was advised that the only way I would get over it was to let them come and see it. In other words, maybe if I sat in it, I would get over it. I allowed them to come for dinner and I thought I was okay as she fed him and sat on his lap. I took it all in and on the chin. I had been doing that for quite some time not realizing it was begrudgingly. I felt like I was doing the right thing.

I had been doing healing work for years, but I'm not sure that my heart was truly repaired. I was angry. Although I had left the marriage, I was angry that he chose to try to get it right for someone else. I felt left with all the parental work and damage, and I resented him for it. Graves' disease and fibroid tumors were the outward expression of what was happening on the inside of me.

Yes, I was the woman in an abusive marriage, and I was still with him off and on after we divorced. I divorced while still in love, and it was so painful. I kept waiting for this grand gesture of therapy and begging to come back home. I would have liked to believe he chose the path of least resistance, but just maybe he chose the path of love.

As time went on, my heart softened, and when our son turned eighteen, my heart shifted. They had a birthday party for King, and it made my heart smile. I just remember walking towards them and thinking when I am around them (or anyone for that matter), I want my presence to bring feelings of love and peace. I had to forgive so that I could bring light when I entered the room.

My heart had suffered so much loss, betrayal, and pain from quite a few people in my life, that I was just tired. From that day on, my motto was "Forgive." Let go of the things that are making me suffer. It's not true love if you are doing it begrudgingly. It hurts, so tend to the wounds and let it go.

Even when I decided that we were done for real, I chose to love him through all of that. He apologized to me multiple times and told me he was sorry that I married an adult and not a man.

DESIGNING THE LIFE I CHOSE

Atlanta Exes marked my official introduction to the public in 2014, although I had made appearances with Lo before and we were featured on *MTV Cribs*, I was not well known. Lo's former road manager, Hank, heard about the opportunity and connected me with the creators Vernon Lynch and Jeff Dyson. I had been offered reality TV opportunities in the past but had always declined. However, after a two-hour conversation with Vernon and Jeff, I surprisingly said yes, this time.

Soon after, I flew to L.A. to meet the producers and the other ladies: Torrei Hart, Tameka Raymond, Monyetta Shaw, and Sheree Buchanan. Right from the start, I made it clear that I was not about the drama — if that was what the show was after, I was not their girl. Before we started filming, the ladies and I met regularly for lunch to build rapport and form a sisterhood. It worked; by the time we started filming, we had truly bonded.

To my surprise, I became a fan favorite on the show. The audience loved my style and personality. I was teased mercilessly for thrifting growing up, but it cultivated my sense of fashion. I was over 200 pounds when we were filming, and everyone would ask when I was doing a fashion line because I was dressed so well, I credit much of that to my wardrobe stylist, Taijuan Wilcox. Thick girls were inspired. "You make me feel like I can wear that," they'd say. Thrifting requires creativity. If you can make some old, mothball-smelling pieces come together and impress folk, then you're talented.

I even met a guy on the show and dated him for a while, though the relationship ended bitterly. The lesson I learned from that experience is to trust your gut, regardless of others' opinions. I had reservations from the start but went against my better judgment.

Despite the show lasting only one season, the recognition and platform it provided have been invaluable. God makes no mistakes, while at the time I had hoped we would be renewed for a second season, I now understand why things panned out the way they did.

After the show, my interior designing business continued to soar. My talents for home décor were initially featured on *MTV Cribs* when I was married, but the recognition from Atlanta Exes helped to catapult my career even further. I still remember the day the crew from *MTV Cribs* came to our home. I was running around making sure that everything was just right. One of the crew members actually told me that it was their second favorite house. I didn't understand why because I had seen some of the most incredible mansions on this show. I absolutely loved our home and was so proud of it, but I wasn't sure what they loved so much in comparison to some of the homes we had seen. I think the energy in the home had something to do with it as well, because I was big on energy clearing and keeping the home as peaceful as I could. I would anoint and pray over every window and doorway, and would sage all closets, cabinets, drawers, and doors. On the day of taping, it was no different — I was running around clearing energy and cleaning windows. The producer said, "We are waiting on you. We want you to do it with him." I looked at my husband and asked, "Is that okay?" I didn't want to do it if it wasn't okay with him. He said, "Of course." He helped me decide what to wear, a ponytail, I put on a brown lip liner and some clear lip gloss and had my first real television debut.

After *MTV Cribs*, our newspaper, the *Atlanta Journal-Constitution* wanted to come to our home to do a spread. They also told us how much they loved our home. At the time, I had already become a certified foot reflexologist and aromatherapist. I was considering going to massage school next. Yet, I was totally addicted to HGTV and was so intrigued by decorating and design.

I remember my husband had decorated the basement a few times, and it just wasn't quite working out the way he wanted. I asked him if I could do it. I drew a very amateur sketch to show him what I had in mind, and he agreed! I was so excited to try out my new skill set. I did a fun and futuristic family space for us. After that, I knew exactly what I wanted to do.

I started a design firm called Inner Piece Design. I was so blessed to have some help from a great guy named Daniel who had an architecture degree. I started decorating homes for friends first. As long as they would pay for the furnishings, I would lend my talents free of charge. I needed to get my feet wet in this industry.

My sister-in-law told me about a successful Black designer who was working on model homes. She gave me her information and told me to call her and see if she would let me shadow her or work under her as an apprentice. Knowing there was someone in the industry who looked like me was exciting. I remember being so amped to call her. In the meantime, I practiced. I read design books and decor magazines and taught myself everything I could.

I knew Ludacris' girlfriend at the time. She made the

introduction, thinking that I could probably help Chris (Ludacris) with a mansion he had purchased.

I thought to myself, *"If this designer helps me, I will give her Chris as a client and then study her every move on this project."* But God had a different plan.

I called the designer and introduced myself. Even though I knew of the projects she was working on, she told me she didn't have anything at the time and she couldn't help me. I was crushed, to say the least, but I wasn't going to let that stop me.

It turned out that Chris "Ludacris" Bridges was meant to be my first paying client. I walked into his massive home, which reminded me of a huge upscale doctor's office. Although I had already seen Ludacris on *Cribs* before, this mansion was a serious upgrade. My mission was to add to that upgrade and make this space breathtaking.

As soon as I walked in, I recognized his dining table right away because I had seen it on *Cribs* at Missy Elliot's house. I pointed it and told him the difference was that the circles on her table *spun*. I also noticed that his living room furniture was the same one on display in a popular furniture store in Buckhead, Georgia. He got upset and said he would call them because they were supposed to take it off the display window.

This set us off on the right foot. He respected my honesty and said that a lot of people around him would just tell him what he wanted to hear. He also let me know that he wasn't ready to decorate. He had a huge crew working outside of his home and he wanted to finish that first.

I was racking my brain, trying to think of how to change his mind, because I knew that he needed help. Although his house was stunning, it needed to feel like a home. So I started pitching a few ideas to him about making his space peaceful so he would feel excited coming home off the road into his custom and curated space.

As our meeting was coming to a close, he showed me a bay window in his kitchen. He asked, "What would you do with this area? This is my favorite place to sit so that I can look out on my lake when I'm having breakfast."

I told him I could build a banquette seating area and make the area cozier for him to have breakfast, relax, and check emails. He said, "Okay, I love that idea. I will let you do this area, and when you're done with that, we will see about moving forward."

I started working with the contractors he already had on site because he obviously trusted them. When we were done, he absolutely loved it.

I remember being at the house one day finishing up that project when I heard his house manager at the time call me over the intercom saying, "Chris is on line one." When I answered the phone, he said, "I love what you did to the great room off the kitchen. How many rooms can you do at a time?"

I said, "As many as you will give me."

That was the beginning of my beautiful career, passion, and God-given gift of interior design. I will always be grateful to Chris for giving me my first real opportunity as a designer. He knew that I was new to the art, but he paid me an amazing rate, he trusted my vision, and he always treated me with integrity, as I saw him do for everyone around him, including his label's artists. Chris was a solid friend to me during the hardest time of my life. He will always be one of my favorite people because of his genuine kindness and strong character.

It's been over twenty years that I have been an interior designer. On a talk show interview with host Dr. Jamal Bryant, I met Devan Carter who was working on the show. He asked the producer of the show how he could reach out to me. When he called, he told me how talented his wife was as a designer. He thought it would be great for her to meet me, being seasoned in the industry. He asked to take me to lunch so I could meet his wife, Phylea. We hit it off immediately, sharing stories about our passion for design, working with people, and travel. She immediately became a close sister-friend.

Brely Evans was shooting a pilot for a new show for me, and Phylea volunteered to come help me with it. That was our first project together. She was a natural on camera, and our design styles complimented perfectly.

After taping the pilot, I called Phy and asked her if she wanted to go into business together. I explained to her that I needed a partner so I could also focus on my life coaching and speaking engagements. She said, "I just asked Devan, do you think Christina would want to go into business together"? I know that sounds crazy, but we both had a love for design, came up with the idea, and it took off. Me and my new business partner started a design firm called Design My Investment during the pandemic and haven't looked back.

We are cultivating beautiful spaces for a diverse clientele all over the United States, and soon to be global. I am so happy to be working in my area of gifting and blessing clients' spaces with a dope, like-minded beautiful soul like Phy.

I Chose to Heal

Here we are, on the third of April, and I have just ended a relationship. My blood pressure is up, and I am sitting in the doctor's office getting my yearly physical with my heart feeling broken. I had just gotten a lung X-ray and it was taking the doctor a long time to come back to the room. I see the X-ray tech walk past my room and now I am internally freaking out.

Finally, Dr. Tyler walks in and says, "Well, your lung X-ray looks good, so that's good." He tells me he is going to put me back on blood pressure meds, then says, "But your EKG is abnormal. We compared this EKG to years prior and it has never looked like this. It looks like maybe your heart has gotten damaged, so I am going to send you to a cardiologist."

Could it be true that my heart is literally broken? I thought to myself, *yes, Christina, it has been broken several times and you keep going, expecting it to tick perfectly.* It is time to make different choices.

In order to break the cycle of abuse, you have to heal from whatever's hurting you. The book *You Can Heal Your Life* by Louise Hay really helped me on my healing journey.

Tony Robbins quotes this saying in one of his talks: "The definition of insanity is doing the same thing over and over and expecting a different result." That is the absolute truth. In order to heal, you have to find another way to do things. "If you do what you always did, you're going to get what you always got."[8] You have to be willing to change direction so that my outcome and everyone that is connected to you will be blessed by it.

You have to do some things differently to get to the destiny that you desire. Even if you don't know what you want right now, you at least know what you don't want. Start setting boundaries so that you don't tolerate the things that bring you pain and discord. If you're tired of how you're feeling in a relationship, you have to establish these boundaries and stand by them, even if that means walking away from someone you love and had planned to spend the rest of your life with. People change. That doesn't mean you have to stick around and suffer until they do. We also have to check ourselves and see how we need to maneuver differently in order to be a better person to the people around us. That's the hardest part.

Some people think that staying busy and forgetting about what's bothering them is the way to heal and move forward in life. However, if you're not willing to face the truth, it will be very hard for you to live a healthy life. Although your life may look good from the outside, those internal struggles shred you on the inside. This leads to faster aging and even illness.

One of my major defining moments occurred in 2009, and I asked myself, *Christina, what are you hungry for?* I had to ask myself this question once I realized all the beautiful clothes I received for Christmas one year prior did not fit on New Year's Day and I had not worn them once!

A few months later, I went to the doctor for my annual physical and was diagnosed with high blood pressure at the level of a very unhealthy older person. However, this did not alarm me too much as I have been given this same diagnosis since I was 28 years old. I was also informed my body was not making enough blood for my heart to pump normally and the physicians needed to understand why this was happening.

After running multiple tests, they discovered one of the culprits, a fibroid tumor that was causing severe anemia in addition to heart palpitations. I was not taking care of myself as much as I should have, but I had recently left my marriage and was so unhappy. I felt I had failed God and my children. Sitting in that doctor's office, and hearing my doctor tell me that I needed to exercise and lose weight, or I would have to take high blood pressure medication for the rest of my life was definitely an eye-opener. I dislike taking Tylenol, so of course there was no chance I was going to take that medicine. I needed to take action quickly to correct this situation.

Without hesitation, I called my personal trainer at the time, Marvel Canada. I knew he would help me achieve the results I needed, as he helped me lose weight after I had my youngest child. When we spoke, I remember asking him, "Marvel, will you help me save my life?"

So, after working out with him for about a month and still eating whatever I wanted, I found myself sitting in a parking lot across the street from my daughter's school, eating a double Philly cheesesteak burger, two chili dogs from Checker's, and large fries from McDonald's.

Let me be clear, this was no average burger; it was a double patty burger with every condiment you can think of on it with Philly cheesesteak meat piled on top of that. The chili dogs were covered in onions and mustard, and I must have wanted those fries from McDonald's because I drove across the street to purchase those. Oh, and let us not forget the ridiculously large strawberry soda that I drank to wash it all down. I was devouring this food so fast, that when I was close to finishing, I started to feel sick.

Sick of myself, because there was no way I was this hungry, but I continued to eat, and tears began to form and stream down my face. At that very moment, I knew I needed to make some serious changes in my life.

This is where my new chapter began. I started with updating my vision board and reading great books to aid in my healing. Some of those books were *You Can Heal Your Life* by Louise Hay, *A New Earth* by Eckhart Tolle, *Eat, Pray, Love* by Elizabeth Gilbert, and the Bible. The book that changed my eating habits and turned me into a vegetarian for five years was a book called *Skinny Bitch*. I bought this book solely based on the shock value of the name. I am human, and I have used profanity since I was in the sixth grade. I still struggle in that area. Funny thing is, I had no idea it was about how we eat.

Along with the books that I was reading, I decided to clean my shoe and wardrobe closets and jewelry boxes and rid my mind and spirit of old anger, resentment, and past pain. What I did not give to my friends or Goodwill, I gave to God. I was strengthening my relationship with God by studying His word, talking to Him, and listening to Him speak to me.

I believe that every illness has some emotional tie. When I was thirty-six, I was diagnosed with Graves' disease. One morning I was in the car taking my son to school and listening to Hot 107.9. Rickey Smiley was playing an inspirational song and then had Pastor Haynes speak. I've been in church since I was a little girl so I've seen people speak in tongues and then someone else would interpret the message from God. I've never been the one to do either. This particular morning, I was so in the spirit from the song and the minister that I was praying and speaking in tongues (some believe it is a heavenly language).

I was sitting in my truck in the driveway parked in front of this beautiful home that my children and I lived in. I started to pray and then came the interpretation of tongues, and the message was, "This is nothing compared to what I am going to give you and where I am going to take you, but no matter how bad things get, stand on my promises."

God is not man so He does not lie! I don't know what it is about us humans, but someone can hear ten great things and the eleventh negative thing is all we will focus on. Needless to say what stood out to me was, "no matter how bad things get." It was scary, even though I heard that it was going to turn out all right.

I had fibroid tumors, so I went to my gynecologist to get my blood tested and have her take a look at the tumors because they had grown so much in the last couple of years. She said, "This thing is huge and it definitely needs to come out so I'm going to have to do surgery. You're so tiny. You've lost a lot of weight and you have a goiter."

I asked her what that was. She asked me if I had problems with my thyroid in the past and I told her my numbers were coming back normal. I always had symptoms of something being wrong, but the doctors could never figure out what it was. They always told me it was anxiety and stress. My hands would shake (tremors), I would be short of breath all the time, I was losing too much weight too fast, my heart was racing, and I would even blackout behind the wheel or while I was walking.

She said, "I'm going to check your thyroid and let you know in a couple of days." I was so nervous waiting for her to call me back. I was answering all my calls on the first ring and nervous as crap.

I sat on my bed and said a prayer. *Lord, use my life as a service to other people. I will do whatever you need me to do.* Not long after that, she called and said, "Sweetheart, your thyroid is extremely overactive. You need to see an internist as soon as possible. I can't do surgery until you get your thyroid numbers under control." I wasn't even sure of what the thyroid's function was. All I knew was that something was wrong, and I needed to combat it right away.

I was so blessed that I had spent the time in the summer changing my lifestyle, the way that I eat, and exercise. I had no idea what my body was about to endure. I decided that I was going to do things the natural and holistic way. So, I studied Dr. Sebi. He was in the business of healing people through natural methods.

My ex-husband was out in L.A and went to Dr. Sebi's store and got me his products. I had purposely lost weight and my body had been exactly where I wanted it to be. Since my thyroid disease had been diagnosed, I continued to drop weight that I did not want to lose. My body was very tiny, and I looked very sick. I remember a few people visiting and looking at me with sadness in their eyes because it was apparent that I was very ill.

I didn't really understand why natural healing wasn't working for me. It was something that I had been doing for years. I did not realize that my condition was so far gone at this point that it was a little too late. The endocrinologist put me on a medication called methimazole. I learned that when your thyroid is overactive it speeds up everything and controls a lot and is connected to my womb, which is where I needed my first initial surgery.

I also learned that I had a tumor so large that it was sitting on my right kidney. The left kidney had to overcompensate meaning it got larger. The doctor kept telling me I was the sickest patient he ever had. He told me I would go into kidney failure before my thyroid was stabilized. They would have to rush me into emergency surgery and I would die from cardiac arrest on the table. By this time, I was stressed out, very tiny, and my weight was very low for my height. You could see the bones protruding out of my shoulders and back. I would fall asleep some days not knowing if I was going to wake up.

I was in Charlotte, North Carolina visiting my sister Paula. I suddenly got a fever of 104.1, it was so debilitating that I could barely get myself to the bathroom. These fevers would continue routinely every two weeks and the closer it got to my surgery several months later, it would happen every few days. The doctors couldn't tell me where the fevers were coming from because they didn't know if it was my kidneys, or something called thyroid storms.

I would leave the doctor's office every week in tears and scared for my life. One particular day, I had gotten to my car to do my normal cry fest every time I left the doctor's office. This time, as I'm crying, I hear a voice saying, "Are you going to believe in the word of man or are you going to stand on my promises?" It took me back to that day in my car listening to Rickey Smiley and praising in the car. I remember saying out loud, *I am going to stand on your promises!*

I decided that I wanted to live, and I was going to stand on the promises of God. So, I started to focus on all that was good instead of putting my energy into what the doctors were saying or on fear and negativity. So every time I would get a fever I would continuously whisper, "Thank you" over and over again because I knew there was a greater purpose to what was happening to me.

This was not just about me, others will also be changed by my illness, my fight, my faith, my resilience, and my healing. I realize that this was my opportunity to start practicing what I preach to everyone else. So, I constantly wrote every night in my gratitude journal, prayed, and started to watch things that were positive and kept my mind on living. I've always been the person who took care of people and made sure their needs were met. Yet when you're ill you can't work, and by not working I couldn't take care of my own needs. Everything was behind and I had no one to call for help that could help.

Lo had been disrespectful to me, and I stopped talking to him initially. After months of being sick and not working, my house was headed into foreclosure. I called and tried to get assistance in any way that I could, but no one came through for help. This is when I started to look for the people that I helped over the years to show up for me. Crickets! So now I started to reevaluate every last friendship that I had.

I've always been somewhat of a loner and my tight circle of

friends was very valuable to me, but some were nowhere to be found. It was also hard to call for help in my time of need. This also became a valuable lesson for me. You shouldn't give everything away and completely deplete yourself.

I also learned that you cannot expect people to do the same things that you would do. People handle things differently than I do. Some people don't handle illness, death, and things of that nature very well, so they don't know what to say or how to say it. Sometimes, it just takes being present for the people you love. There would be days when I couldn't make it out of my bed in time and would vomit and use the bathroom everywhere. It was extremely humbling to have your nine-year-old son helping you get back and forth to the bathroom.

Another valuable lesson I learned during this time was a closed mouth doesn't get fed. I was sitting in the house counting all the people who hadn't shown up, but never asked for help, hiding so others wouldn't see me sick because I thought I was protecting them. What can I say, I am a Taurus and I am stubborn.

I started speaking up and asking for help. Whether it was someone to bring food, water, or to help me clean. During this time, my first love Eric was back in the picture and was taking care of me.

Kalah's dad was also back in her life. I remember one day, both of them picked me up and took me to the bathroom. Talk about the past repeating itself. The men who loved me as a young girl were sent back to assist me as a woman. The Most High came through and I was able to keep my home. Lo and I eventually became cordial again, he stepped in and paid all of my medical bills and eventually got health insurance for me. He was still caring for me after five years of being divorced.

Ironically, I lost my womb, the root of how I spent my younger days looking for someone to love me. When I got sick, I stopped doing my design work for years because I lost all my energy and motivation. To this day, I believe my disease was caused by me not facing my unaddressed issues head-on.

One thing I've found that gets in the way of my healing is that I worry too much about how I make other people feel. I find myself asking God, "Why did you have to make my heart so breakable?" I've learned that the hard way. I can still care about other people, but I have to put myself first if I'm going to allow myself to heal.

I have also realized that illness is tied to the energy we put out. Now, I try to live with intentionality. I choose love, peace, and joy. I don't want to be petty because you get what you give. If you give negativity, gossip, pettiness, that's what you're going to get.

So many people adopt a victim mentality and ask, "Why is stuff always happening to me?" You have to look at how you talk and act. When you put energy out into the world, that's what you're calling into your life, and you have to take accountability for it. Whenever I am going through something now, I ask God, *"What in this is supposed to be the lesson?"*

Coming into the world with the knowledge that I came to do something special was the only clarity I had going through this life experience. Earlier in this journey, I started to feel like I couldn't make any mistakes. Although I know God would love and forgive me, I never wanted to disappoint him.

When I would do things that I knew were referred to as "sin," I would crucify myself. I already felt unworthy and like I wasn't enough. I was raised in a fear-based religion that taught me guilt and shame. I was told I was loved, but if I made mistakes, I would burn eternally. So, I tried my best not to ever make any mistakes.

I remember standing in Dr. Sue Carter-Collins' kitchen while she made me hot tea, and explaining to her how I didn't want to disappoint God and how I didn't want him to be mad at me for not getting things right. Dr. Sue paused and said, "The first thing we are going to do is reconcile your relationship with God because he is not mad at you. God is love."

She shared with me how we choose our parents and choose to have these experiences. This was my first of many hours-long appointments with gut-wrenching and powerful healing sessions that were life-altering for me. Healing has been a journey, not a destination.

Holistic healing is not for the faint of heart. It is a healing journey you have to be willing to feel the intensity of re-living the pain and aches of your mistakes over and over again until the body does what it was gifted to do and that is to eventually heal itself, physically, emotionally, and spiritually.

Since October 2022, I have stopped eating meat and have been very consistent with meditation. I would meditate in the steam sauna every morning and pray daily. So, by the time my EKG was abnormal, I was already in healing mode.

At this point, it was time to heal in every area of my life. We all have issues that we need to heal. Yet, with all the healing work I've done over the years, I was trying to figure out how I got to the place where my heart had literally broken and I could feel that it was time to face all of my heartaches. That did not mean calling up everyone who hurt me and expressing myself.

I went back to the most natural thing for me since I was young: journaling. With the advice of my therapist, Mikell Rozier, I went down the list of all my losses. Whether it was friendships, family, or love relationships I needed to write down all of the feelings that I had going on with me. I expressed my pain on pieces of paper.

I decided I wanted to revere The Most High by praying on my knees in the morning and at night. After prayer, I do my meditation. What I know for sure is, praying is when we are petitioning The Most High and meditation is when we can hear clearly from Him.

I thought about how I had almost completely avoided the pandemic until the summer before these diagnoses. Maybe it was COVID-19 that did physical damage, I have no idea. Every disease has an emotional tie. What emotional tie could have caused this? According to Louise L. Hay, the probable cause is, it represents the center of love and security.

I must admit, I had never really felt safe being loved by others because I had always expected that they would hurt me. I immediately thought back on every relationship I've had, the way I have been treated, the way I have treated others, and what energies I had been attracting.

Turning fifty started ushering in some real open and honest realizations. My family and friends came together and gave me a surprise birthday party. It was absolutely beautiful. My family and friends together, that hadn't happened since my wedding, and my paternal family wasn't there so this was monumental for me. I asked everyone to circle around me and pray for my heart. In that moment, I felt my healing was done.

I was supposed to take a trip to Bali, Indonesia, and spend a month, but plans had to change. The day after my birthday party, I had to get a heart monitor put on and wear it for thirty days. After the echocardiogram and stress echo, I was told I had leaky valves, and my aorta (main artery) was dilated (enlarged). The enlarged aorta can cause a heart aneurysm. Which is how my grandmother Christine died at thirty-seven.

I found out after wearing the monitor that the top and bottom of my heart were beating differently and not in sync like they normally do. During the thirty days of wearing the monitor, my heart stopped for six seconds. I was sent to a heart rhythm specialist, and he told me I would probably be on a pacemaker in 5 to 10 years.

He said I may have to have a very invasive and painful surgery if this wasn't caused by sleep apnea. My sleep apnea test came back normal. The Most High always has the last word.

I gave myself a day to cry my eyes out, I was scared. I fell to my knees and started praying and surrendering everything to The Most High. I told Him, I was here for His will, and I would do whatever He needed me to do, even if that meant my time on earth was up.

After standing up, I decided to keep enjoying life—dancing, designing, and working on all my gifts—and I soft-launched my new accessory business. I had already stopped eating meat and was eating mostly raw, plant-based food.

One day, I was scrolling on the gram and I saw a video that Yah'ki Awakened posted on the healing power of watermelon on the heart. That day I decided that I was going to fast on watermelon only.

So, my sister Chelle and I took a trip to Mexico for her birthday, and as soon as we got back to Atlanta, I started my fast. It was the same day I was going to see the thoracic specialist. He explained to me that I needed to get a CT scan with contrast to take a closer look at my heart.

The appointment was set for over a month away. All I ate was seeded watermelon, took @yahkiawakened herbs, drank watermelon juice, water, coconut water, got in the steam sauna at least five days a week, sun-gazed, grounded for three to four days, and went to Effect Fitness three days a week (the cardiologist said I could work out three days a week).

I felt like all of my senses were heightened, and my spiritual awareness was so clear. After I finished this fast, I ate seeded grapes and oranges next. The watermelon was fairly easy for me because it is so filling, and I love the taste. We grew up on watermelon, so it wasn't as hard as I thought it was going to be.

A couple of weeks into the watermelon fast, the heart palpitations stopped, and my high blood pressure started lowering. I was starting to feel better than I had in a long time. So, in the last week of my watermelon fast, I went to get my CT scan done. I ended the watermelon fast and did seven days on seeded grapes, and then seven days on oranges, and other astringent fruits, and eventually broke my fast with raw veggies.

My blood pressure had gotten so low that the cardiologist took me off of my blood pressure medications. I couldn't believe how amazing I felt physically, spiritually, and emotionally. My CT scan came back *beautiful!* Everything was normal—even the size of my aorta. I feel like I am aging backwards.

Life for me has changed. Not only do I feel great, but I am eating beautiful, colorful foods, traveling, working on my gifts, enjoying my children, and grandchildren, and I feel great emotionally. I'm dating again and my life has balance.

I no longer care about what others think. I know who I am now. This is a feeling I have desired my whole life. Here I am turning fifty years old, and I am starting over completely. I want to go back to The Most High empty. I want to tell Him that I utilized all of the gifts that He gave me, took all the chances I was afforded, and let Him know that I did the work and worked out every kink in my chain that I could.

I love me and I choose me. I am proud of myself for this new way of life. I give all the glory to the Most High God. It is my choice!

CONCLUSION

As I reflect on my journey, what I've grown to understand is that every path I've taken, and every outcome I've faced, stems from my choices. "My Choice to Choose" isn't just a title; it's a testament to the power we hold over our lives. Was it easy to move away from the patterns that I saw growing up? Heck no, I had to be intentional about creating a different life.

I've broken generational curses, confronted my deepest wounds, and embraced healing in its most beautiful form. Deferred dreams are not dreams denied; they are opportunities waiting to be realized. Success, to me, isn't merely about achieving goals, it's about forging a life of purpose and contentment. Peace is my holy grail, it's my North Star — I seek it every day.

My journey has been a blend of triumphs and tribulations, but all of it has contributed to the woman that I am today. The life that I am living now is proof that regardless of circumstances, you have the power to change your life. I did, and you can too.

ENDNOTES

1. Buchanan, Edna. "Edna Buchanan (20+ Sourced Quotes)." Lib Quotes. Accessed December 12, 2022. https://libquotes.com/edna-buchanan.

2. White, R.L. Speech honoring Martin Luther King Jr. January 20, 2014. Anderson, South Carolina.

3. Buchanan, Laurie, and Laurie Buchanan. Tuesdays with Laurie, 9AD. Accessed November 2, 2023. https://tuesdayswithlaurie.com/.

4. Hughes, Langston. "Mother to Son." Poets.org, February 4, 2021. https://poets.org/poem/mother-son.

5. Scriptures marked RSV are from the Revised Standard Version of the Bible, copyright © 1946, 1952, and 1971 the Division of Christian Education of the National Council of the Churches of Christ in the United States of America. Used by permission. All rights reserved.

6. Scriptures marked KJV are from the Holy Bible, King James Version. All rights reserved.

7. Gillette, Hope. "How to Recognize an Emotionally Unavailable Parent." Psych Central, May 19, 2022. https://psychcentral.com/relationships/signs-of-having-an-emotionally-unstable-unavailable-parent#defining-it.

8. Badu, Erykah. Cleva. Motown Records, 202, Accessed April 12, 2024. https://open.spotify.com/track/1GoTvQP3JEeA8oh5I9b2xc.

9. Potter, Jessie. "The Milwaukee Sentinel," October 24, 1981. "Search for Quality Called Key to Life" by Tom Ahern. Accessed on Quote Investigator, https://quoteinvestigator.com/2016/04/25/get/#r+13559+1+2.

ACKNOWLEDGMENTS

To the beautiful loves of my life, Sierra, Kalah, and Kingston: Love is an action word and I pray that I have and am loving you in action. You all are my reason. I love you!

To my five grandchildren: I had no idea that my heart had the capacity to stretch so big until each of you were born, and every time it expanded even more. The only difference between me and your mom is that I didn't give birth to you. The love is the same as if I did. Tru-Fighter you were born with an old-soul full of love and you are going to change the world. Isabella (Izzy), you have the most beautiful heart I've seen. Kató-Wulf, you are so wonderful and intelligent. Avery, you are full of love and will make a great impact on the world in a great way. Amaia-Madilyn (Maddie Cakes), you are a genius.

To my loves who are no longer with us: My dad, Melvin Campbell; my sister, Ursula Armstrong; and my friends, Shenelle Evans, Shayna Odom, and Taijuan Wilcox. I love and miss you all so very much. Thank you all for your contributions to my life. May God rest your souls.

To my wonderful siblings, we are connected by DNA, memories, and love: Kamarey Grissett, Nakemia Grissett, Tony Campbell, Keyata Gable Lindsay, Stacey Whitehead, Paula Campbell, Chevelle Campbell, and Biannca Davis—I love you all, and thank you for loving me.

ABOUT THE AUTHOR

Christina Johnson epitomizes resilience and metamorphosis. Born into challenging circumstances, she defied expectations, forging her path from teen motherhood to entrepreneurial success. Moving to Atlanta in pursuit of her creative dreams, fate intervened, leading her to a partnership with a world-renowned Grammy award-winning artist, which eventually ignited a quest for inner peace and a commitment to advocacy against domestic violence. As muse and mother of three, Johnson's journey evolved, culminating in the co-founding of "Design My Investment," an interior design firm recognized for its fusion of transitional elegance and unconventional style.

From reality TV stardom on VH1's "Atlanta Exes" to battling Graves' disease, Christina's tenacity has shone through. Now a global master certified professional life coach and mentor, she motivates women worldwide through personalized coaching, group programs, and events.

Johnson's story embodies triumph over adversity, inspiring others to practice self-love, forgiveness, and authentic living— a modern-day superwoman embracing her purpose and helping others realize their power to do the same.

Photo Credit: Drea Nicole
Makeup Artist: Joyua Gibson

Learn more at www.christinasjohnson.com or

scan the QR code below.

Photo Credit: Art Terrell Photography

Photo Credit : Derek Blanks

www.ingramcontent.com/pod-product-compliance
Lightning Source LLC
Chambersburg PA
CBHW051144120626
46547CB00012B/937